TALES OF OLD
MANILA

Memories from the Past of Asia's Most Colorful City

Lisa Angstadt

"Give me ten thousand Filipino soldiers
and I will conquer the world."

Douglas MacArthur

Tales of Old Manila

By Lisa Angstadt

ISBN-13: 978-988-8422-08-1

This book has been reset in 10pt Book Antiqua. Spellings and punctuations are left as in the original edition.

HIS048000 HISTORY / Asia / Southeast Asia

EB078

Published by Earnshaw Books Ltd. (Hong Kong).

The Tales Books

The concept of our Tales series of books is "history with all the juicy bits highlighted and all the boring bits removed," a curated and easily digestible pot pourri of historical oddities, stories and information from a city's past. A pastiche of quotes, extracts and old images, with some explanation along the way. It is a selective choice and somewhat random, certainly not completist. The material is laid out roughly chronologically, but you can open the book anywhere and start reading. Historical cliches are revived and addressed with glee. Virtually nothing strays over two pages. Please enjoy the feast.

The materials in the book come from a myriad sources. If any item is attributed inappropriately, please let us know and we will correct it. We believe all materials are either out of copyright or used within the bounds of fair usage. We are happy to remove any items where this proves not to be the case.

Other Books in the Tales Series

A Sherman tank under the ruined arch entrance of Fort Santiago in February 1945

Chronology

900	The kingdom of Tondo, covering much of Luzon Island, including today's Manila, established, an Indianized Hindu-Buddhist culture
1240	An Arab trader Tuan Masha'ika, introduces Islam to the Sulu Islands, part of today's southern Philippines
1457	Sultanate of Sulu founded by Sayyid Abubakar Abirin, an Arab-Muslim explorer
1500	Brunei invades Tondo, sets up "Kingdom of Maynila"
1521	Ferdinand Magellan reaches the Philippine Islands (March 31). Magellan killed by Lapu-Lapu, the ruler of Mactan (April 27)
1525-1536	Attempted expeditions to the Philippines by Spain, all failed
1543	Spanish explorer Ruy Lopez de Villalobos leads a successful expedition and names the islands of Samar and Leyte as Las Islas Filipinas in honor of the crown prince of Spain, Philip of Asturias
1565	Miguel Lopez de Legazpi arrives in the Philippines (February 13) Legazpi establishes the first permanent Spanish settlement in Cebu (May 8)

A postcard from the 1960s. The greeting word "Mabuhay" means "long life" in Tagalog

Escolta Street in the Binondo district of Manila, in 1905

1571	Legazpi moves the Spanish colonial government from Cebu to Manila
1574	Chinese pirate captain Limahong attacks Manila, fails to take it
1579	Roman Catholic Diocese of Manila established
1587-1588	Conspiracy of the Maharlikas, a plot against Spanish colonial rule by Tagalog noblemen the uprising failed
1593	*Doctrina Christiana* is published in Tagalog and Spanish, believed to be the first book printed in the Philippines
1600	The Manila Galleon trade between Manila and Acapulco in Mexico begins, continued until 1815
1602	Revolt of Chinese residents, known as Sangley Rebellion, put down by the Spaniards with the help of the Japanese and Filipinos. An estimated 20,000 people were slaughtered
1611	University of Santo Tomas established, the first university in the Philippines. originally a Catholic seminary
1645	Massive earthquake hits Luzon Island, causing massive damage in Manila and large numbers of deaths including 600 Spaniards

1762	British fleet seizes Manila Bay as part of Seven Years' War (Sept 22), Manila falls under British rule (October 5), Dawsonne Drake becomes first British Governor-General (Nov 2)
1764	British occupation ends
1788	Birth of the greatest Tagalog poet, Francisco "Balagtas" Baltazar
1837	Manila declared an open port
1863	Earthquake leaves Manila in ruins
1863	Another earthquake causes huge damage in Manila
1872	Around 200 Filipino soldiers and workers at Fort San Felipe mutiny with the aim of starting a national uprising against Spanish rule. The attempt fails
1887	Filipino nationalist José Rizal's novel *Noli Me Tangere* (Latin for 'Touch me Not') published, exposing the inquities of the Spanish Catholic priests and colonial administrators. It is today obligatory reading for high school students
1896	José Rizal executed on charges of rebellion. Considered one of the greatest heroes of the Philippines
1898	United States declares war on Spain (April 26), Admiral Dewey sinks Spanish fleet in Manila Bay (May 1), US troops arrive (July 17). Resistance from Filipino fighters continues until 1903

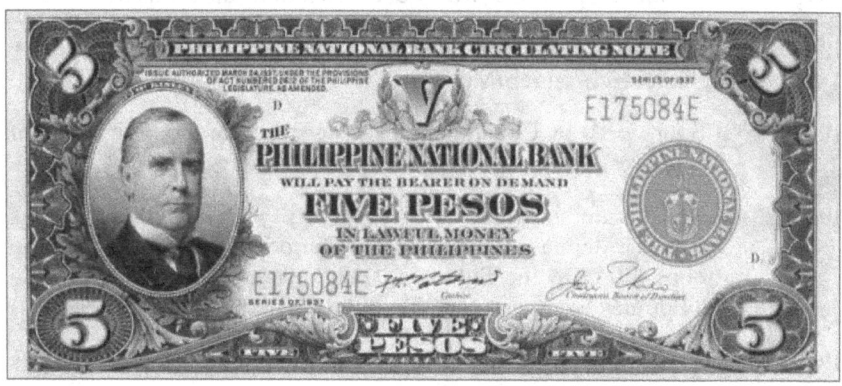

Five peso banknote issued in 1937, during the American administration

7

The Pasig River around the year 1900

1901	Balangiga massacre, in which the US 9th Infantry were attacked by townspeople, resulting in 48 dead
1908	The University of the Philippines established in Manila
1930	The Communist Party of the Philippines established
1935	The Philippine Constitution is signed and the Philippine Commonwealth is inaugurated
1941	General Douglas MacArthur declares Manila an open city
1942	Japanese troops enter Manila (Jan 4), MacArthur leaves (March 11), US forces surrender (May 6)
1944	US forces led by General Doulas MacArthur land on the island of Leyte (Oct 20)
1945	US troops land in large numbers (January 9), US and Filipino troops recapture Manila (March 3), 16,000 US troops and 330,000 Japanese troops killed in the fighting, Japan surrenders (August 15), the Philippines becomes a member of the United Nations (October)
1946	US recognizes the Independence of the Republic of the Philippines

1950	The Philippines joins the Korean War on the side of the Allies
1965	Ferdinand Marcos takes office as President
1968	Jabidah massacre; alleged killing of Moro soldiers by members of the Philippines armed forces
1969	Miss Philippines Gloria Diaz, crowned Miss Universe
1972	Marcos imposes Martial Law
1974	The last Japanese soldier in the Philippines surrenders
1975	"Thrilla in Manila" Muhammad Ali vs. Joe Frazier boxing match
1981	Martial Law lifted
1983	Opposition leader Benigno Aquino assassinated at Manila Airport on his return from exile
1986	"People's Revolution" demonstrations against Marcos (February)
1986	The Marcos' leave Philippines for Hawaii (Feb 25)
1989	Ferdinand Marcos dies

Santa Cruz Church and Plaza, late 19th century

DE STAD MANILHA

A copper plate engraving showing a map of Manila, created in 1726 by Valentijn

The
Spanish
Era
And
Before

The Big Picture

The Philippines is an archipelago of 7,107 islands to the southeast of the Asian landmass with a total area of 300,000 square kilometers. The largest islands are Luzon and Mindanao. The capital Manila is located on the west coast of Luzon.

Map of the Philippines from 1774

From Whence Manila

Manila is derived from two Tagalog words, "may," meaning "there is," and "nilad," the name of a shrub that once grew abundantly along the banks of the Pasig River and the shores of Manila Bay. Maynilad, or "where the nilad grows," was a prosperous Islamic town ruled by Rajah Sulayman, descendant of a royal Malay family, when the Spanish took the region in the 1570s.

An idyllic representation of traditional Philippines village life from the early 19th century

The True Manila

A description of the Intramuros section of the city from A Day in "The Very Noble City," Manila: A lecture by Clay MacCauley, *published in The Japan Gazette in 1899*

At the right continued, as far as we went, those forbidding ramparts. They gradually inclined from the river, back of a widening quat and the spacious Plaze de Magallanes, showing thereby only the more fully the overtopping towers, spires and domes of the palaces, churches, monasteries and colleges crowded together behind them. There lay the true Manila, the Manila of centurys past, wherein has centered Spain as State Church and School.

The Kingdom of Tondo

Tondo was a kingdom that ruled large parts of Luzon Island, including today's Manila, from around 900AD to the arrival of the Spanish in the 16th century. The culture was influenced by the Indian-related culture that spread across Asia prior to the arrival of Islam to Java, Borneo and Cambodia, all of which had ties with Tondo. The kingdom used a Sanskrit-related script, and the oldest-known document in the Philippines, the Laguna Copperplate, is written in this language. In the document, the Lady Angkatan and her brother are forgiven a debt. The document translates as:

Long Live! In the Year of Saka 822, month of Waisakha, according to the astronomer. The fourth day of the waning moon, Monday. On this occasion, Lady Angkatan, and her relative whose name is Bukah, the children of the Honourable Namwaran, were awarded a document of complete pardon from the Commander-in-Chief of Tundun, represented by the Lord Minister of Pailah, Jayadewa. This means that, through the Honourable Scribe, the Honourable Namwaran is totally cleared of his salary-related debts of 1 Kati and 8 Suwarna, before the Honorable Lord Minister of Puliran, Kasumuran; by the authority of the Lord Minister of Pailah, represented by Ganasakti. The Honourable and widely-renowned Lord Minister of Binwagan, represented by Bisruta. And, with his whole family, upon ordered of the Lord Minister of Dewata, represented by the Chief of Mdang, because of his loyalty as a subject of the Commander-in-Chief. Therefore, the living descendants of the Honorable Namwaran are cleared of all debts of the Honourable Namwaran to the Lord Minister of Dewata. This, in any case, whosoever, sometime in the future, who shall state that the debt is not yet cleared of the Honourable...

laguna copperplate inscription

14

Dividing The Cake of Souls

A decree from the King of Spain in 1594 to the Governor of the Philippines, Gomez Perez Dasmariftas, giving different Catholic orders exclusive rights in different parts of the Philippines, in order to avoid contests for the souls of the locals.

To Gomez Perez Dasmariftas, knight of the order of Santiago, my governor and captain-general of the Filipinas Islands. After reading what you wrote me recently in regard to the need of those islands for religious to carry out our obligation to the conversion and instruction of the natives, I have ordered the needful despatch put thereto, so that at the present one hundred religious are going there-to wit, forty Augustinians, twenty-four Dominicans, eighteen descalced Franciscans, and eighteen of the Society. Furthermore, additional missionaries shall be sent until the need is met. Now because I have learned that better results will be obtained by assigning each order to a district by itself, and more emulation will ensue among them without their embarrassing one another, or their work overlapping, as might happen if they were assigned to districts regardless of order, I command you, together with the bishop of those islands, to divide the provinces, for the said instruction and conversion, among the religious of the orders, in such a manner that where Augustinians go there shall be no Franciscans, nor religious of the Society where there are Dominicans. Thus you will proceed, assigning each order to its province; taking note that the province allotted to the Society must have the same manner of instruction as the others; for this same obligation rests upon them there as upon the others, and it does not at all differ from them. Given at Aranjuez, April 27, one thousand five hundred and ninety-four.

I, THE KING

Countersigned by Don Luis de Salazar and approved by the Council

A square in old Manila, probably in the 1890s. Note the horse-drawn trams.

Missing the Boat

Ferdinand Magellan, a Portuguese sea captain born in 1480, was chosen by King Charles I of Spain to search for a westward route to the "Spice Islands." He set sail in 1519 with a fleet of five ships, headed south to the tip of South America, passing through the Strait of Magellan, and into the waters he named the Pacific Ocean. They arrived at the Philippine Islands in 1521, and set out to convert the locals to Christianity. They succeeded in converting the Rajah Humabon, ruler of the island of Cebu, on whose advice Magellan then sailed to the island of Mactan adjacent to Cebu, to convert the ruler, Lapu Lapu. When Magellan and his crew landed on the beach, they were attacked and Magellan was killed. The rest of the crew continued westwards and became the first human beings to circumnavigate the globe.

Ferdinand Magellan

Slayer of Spaniards, Lapu-Lapu

Lapu-Lapu

Lapu-Lapu was a chieftain on the island of Mactan, just to the east of today Cebu City, and he and his men attacked Ferdinand Magellan's landing party on the beach at dawn on April 27, 1521, killing Magellan. Some reports say Lapu-Lapu was born in Borneo, but the standard Filipino sagas would definitely have him as a son of the Philippine islands. He is today revered as a hero, the first man to stand up against the colonial Spaniard invaders. His name also belongs to a fish of the grouper variety, which is very tasty, especially if you're Spanish.

The Death of an Adventurer

The following is a graphic and probably accurate account of the death of Ferdinand Magellan at the hands of Lapu-Lapu and his warriors on the beach at Mactan, taken from The Voyage of Magellan, *the Journal of Antonio Pigafetta, published in 1874 by the Hakluyt Society in London*

The natives continued to pursue us, and picking up the same spear four or six times, hurled it at us again and again. Recognizing the captain, so many turned upon him that they knocked his helmet off his head twice, but he always stood firmly like a good knight, together with some others. Thus did we fight for more than one hour, refusing to retire farther. An Indian hurled a bamboo spear into the captain's face, but the latter immediately killed him with his lance, which he left in the Indian's body. Then, trying to lay hand on sword, he could draw it out but halfway, because he had been wounded in the arm with a bamboo spear. When the natives saw that, they all hurled themselves upon him. One of them wounded him on the left leg with a large cutlass, which resembles a scimitar, only being larger. That caused the captain to fall face downward, when immediately they rushed upon him with iron and bamboo spears and with their cutlasses, until they killed our mirror, our light, our comfort, and our true guide. When they wounded him, he turned back many times to see whether we were all in the boats. Thereupon, beholding him dead, we, wounded, retreated, as best we could, to the boats, which were already pulling off.

Magellan's flagship, the Victoria

A portrayal of Magellan's death

17

Legazpi

Ferdinand Magellan visit the Philippines in 1521 and claimed the islands for the king of Spain, but it was another four decades before the Spanish came back. In 1565, the Conquistador Miguel Lopez de Legazpi, arrived with 400 soldiers and sailors after a voyage across the Pacific from Mexico, which he called New Spain, to establish the colony of the Spanish East Indies. He first established a settlement at Cebu, and attacked and took the northern island of Luzon in 1570. Legazpi chose Manila to be the colonial capital in 1571 and crucially initiated the annual Manila galleon trips from Spain's possession of Mexico on the other side of the Pacific. The galleons brought silver, which was the main currency for trade with China and the rest of East Asia. Spanish silver bought Chinese porcelain and silk as well as spices including nutmeg and other precious commodities which were

Miguel López de Legazpi, the first Governor of the Spanish Philippines, 1565 to 1572

shipped to Europe for re-sale. This intercontinental trade, with Manila at its hub, effectively bankrolled the Spanish Empire. The city of Legaspi on the southeast tip of Luzon Island is named after him.

An Oil painting of Manila on the inside of a wooden chest, circa 1640-50. Museo de Arte Jose Luis Bello, Peubla. Mexico. After the 1645 earthquake Manila was reconstructed. By the end of the 17th century, Intramuros had some six hundred houses that were protected by its stone walls

Chinese Rifles

The text of a letter from Legazpi to the King of Spain, Philip II, reporting on the progress of the establishment of the Spanish East Indies. The translation was published in Volume 2 of the magnificent compendium of Philippine source materials, The Philippine Islands, by Emma Blair and James Alexander Robertson, published in 1903.

Very exalted and powerful Lord: At the end of the year one thousand five hundred and sixty-four, I left Nueva Espana by way of the South Sea, for the discovery of these islands of the West, by order and commission of his majesty; and having arrived at these Filipinas Islands, I sent a vessel back to Nueva Espana to discover the return route, and to give his majesty an account of the voyage, and inform him that a colony had been settled in this island of Cubu. What has happened since then is, that in these fortunate times of his majesty and your highness there have been discovered and are being discovered many island and lands, in which God, our Lord, and his majesty and your highness may be very well please with the great growth of our holy Catholic faith. And, not to be prolix with long relations of affairs and details concerning this land, I will refer you to those which I am writing to the royal Council of the Indies. It seemed to me that your highness would be please with specimens of the weapons with which these natives fight; a Chinese arquebuse, of which there are some among these natives. Although they are very dexterous in handling these guns, when on the sea aboard of their praus, they carry them more to terrify than to kill. And likewise they bring you a half-dozen lances and another half-dozen daggers, a cutlass, two corselets, two helmets, and a bow with quiver and arrows, all which they use. Moreover, that your highness may see how scrupulous these people are in their dealings, I send your highness a pair of balances and one of their steelyards. I beg humbly your highness to receive my desire to serve you ever as a faithful servant, and pardon my boldness. Very exalted and powerful lord, may our Lord watch over the very exalted and powerful and royal person of your highness, and may he augement you with more kingdoms and seignories for many and fortunate years. From this island of Cubu, July 15, 1567. Your highness's very faithful servant who kisses your royal hands.

- Miguel Lopez de Legazpi

"Of course, he goes first to the Escolta; in fact, no matter where he wants to go, he usually passes through this thoroughfare, the busiest, most interesting street in all Manila"

American traveler Burton Holmes on Escolta Street

The Catholics are Coming

The priests arrived, of course, with Magellan in 1521 and started the effort of converting and civilizing the unenlightened masses immediately. The story of the next five centuries is checkered, but the result is that over 80% of people in the Philippines today are Roman Catholics, and the country is the third-largest Catholic country in the world after Brazil and Mexico. The only other country in Asia that has a Christian majority is East Timor. The first Mass in the islands was held with Magellan in attendance on Easter Sunday, March 31, 1521.

Bet Hedging

The Civilizers of The Philippines, *published the Catholic city of Boston in 1903, described the arrival of Catholicism in the islands:*

"Among the first Missionaries, who are entitled to the honour of having propagated the Christian Faith in the Philippine Islands, must be mentioned the Secular Priests, who, as Chaplains, accompanied Magallanes on his first expedition in 1521. Owing to their preaching and treatment in Cebu, they made a great many converts who, together with their Chief Hamabar and about 800 of the Principals of the Tribe, were baptized."

A detail of Carlos V. Francisco's "First Mass in the Philippines" painting

Thomas Cavendish, English Pirate

The book An Historical View of The Philippine Islands *by Martinez de Zuñiga, published in 1814, has the following description of the activities of Thomas Cavendish, an English sea captain – some would say pirate – who in 1587 captured the Manila galleon* Santa Anna *off the coast of what is today California. The Spanish galleon was on its way to Manila loaded with a cargo primarily of gold and silver. Cavendish then sailed across the Pacific and in early 1588 attacked the Spanish settlement on the island of Iloilo, south of Manila. He and his ship made it safely home to London later that year. Interestingly, this extract is entirely wrong about Cavendish's movements.*

Aemulus æquorei, admiratorque Draconis
Commodiore via, et ʃpacijs breuioribus Orbem
Circumagens, patriam multa cum laude reuiʃi;
Pluraque Neptuno et digniʃima Marte peregi.
Si Mare Cretensis neʃcit, tum neʃciet Anglus
Oceanum, et viuet poʃiris ingloruus armis.

"Among the calamities which happened during this government, the loss of the ship Santa Anna was not the least; she was on her way, richly laden, to Acapulco, and was taken by the English. Cavendish, an English pirate, emulous of the fame of Drake, having equipped five ships, with the assistance of Queen Elizabeth, took his departure for this quarter of the world; and having committed many acts of hostility on the coasts of Brazil and Peru, he arrived at Molucca, where he procured every information respecting the produce of the Philippines, and the rich cargoes which every year were sent from these islands to Acapulco. Well instructed, likewise, in the tract observed by our galleons, he sailed for the coast of California, to lie in wait for the annual ship destined for New Spain. In due time the Santa Anna, as is customary, made her appearance on that coast, in prosecution of her voyage to Acapulco, and fell into the hands of the English without any resistance, being quite unprepared."

The Manila Galleons

A description of the trade linking Manila and New Spain - that is, Mexico - for over 200 years, as given in the book, The Manila-Acapulco Galleons *by Shirley Fish, published in 2011*

During the sixteenth to the nineteenth centuries, the trans-Pacific treasure galleons sailed annually from Manila to Acapulco. In Manila, the vessel was loaded with the scented spices of the East, luxurious silks from China, exquisite hand crafted lacquerware from Japan and a multitude of Oriental goods that the Spaniards of New Spain longed to own. The returning galleon from Acapulco to Manila, carried as much as 2.5 million silver pesos in payment of the goods sent to the New Spain in the previous year, as well as a yearly silver subsidy of 250,000 reales for the maintenance of the colonial government in the Philippines. But while the galleons mainly sailed alone and unaccompanied from Manila to Acapulco and vice versa, they were vulnerable to a host of calamities and misfortunes. A fire on board the vessel or a terrifying storm could end the voyage and the lives of everyone on the ship even before the galleon was able to reach land. Additionally, the commanders of the galleons were always threatened by lurking pirates and privateers who preyed on the vessels and coveted the treasures they carried.

Calle del Rosario in the late 19th century.

An illustration of a battle between a British warship and a Spanish galleon.

HMS Centurion Hits a Galleon

The heavily-loaded Manila galleons were always targets for attacks, and the British ship HMS Centurion attacked the Spanish galleon Nuestra Senhora de Capadongo off the coast of the Philippines at Cape Espiritu Santo on June 20, 1748. After a cannon battle which left 67 Spanish dead and two dead on the British ship. The British commander, George Anson, then took the Spanish ship to the Chinese port of Canton and sold it.

The British are Coming

The Seven Years War, between 1756 and 1763, was one of the many tedious wars that Europe endured over the centuries, but it was special because it was the first truly global war, fought on all continents. On one side were France and Spain and on the other Britain and Prussia. The British used the opportunity to attack the Spanish forces in Manila in 1762. The campaign was led by Colonel William Draper, the commanding officer of the 79th Regiment of Foot, then stationed in Madras in British-controlled India. The British easily beat the Spanish and occupied Manila and nearby Cavite for about two years, but never tried to take over the rest of the Philippines. They handed control back to the Spanish in 1764, according to the terms of the Treaty of Paris.

William Draper

An excerpt from William Draper's journal

On the twenty-third of September we anchored in Manila Bay; and soon found, that our visit was unexpected; the Spaniards were unprepared. To increase as much as possible the visible confusion and consternation of the enemy, we determined to lose no time in the attack on the port of Cavite, that was at first intended, but proceed directly to the grand object, judging that our conquest there would of course oc-

Battle of Manila 1762

casion and draw after it the fall of Cavite. On the morning of the twenty-fourth, we sent an effectual summons to the town, and, with the Admiral and other principal officers, examined the coast, in order to fix upon a proper spot for landing troops, artillery and stores.

The First Sunday

An excerpt from Escape to Manila, *by Frank Ephraim, on how the few Jewish refugees from Nazi Germany who made it to the Philippines were treated by the local jewish community.*

Manila offered many pleasures, most of which the refugees could not afford. But every newly-arrived Jewish refugee was taken to Dewey Boulevard on their first Sunday in Manila. The boulevard, a magnificent combination of recreation park, thoroughfare, meeting place, and lookout point, fronted Manila Bay. There the refugees strolled, and newcomers were introduced to "old timers" who had arrived only a few months earlier. One of the joys on Dewey Boulevard were the Magnolia ice cream vendors. They pushed their yellow carts along the length of the boulevard and sold their least expensive product - a chocolate-flavored popsicle - to most of their customers. These ice cream vendors were at the top of the vendor hierarchy, above the Filipinos who peddled candy - Hershey bars, Three Musketeers, Milky Ways, and other American confections - but the refugees could identify with all the vendors because the items for sale were beyond the means of refugees and vendors alike.

> "Except for self-interest, we are mutually contrary and hateful."
> *The Spanish governor Luis Perez Dasmariñas in a missive to the Spanish king on June 28, 1597, commenting on the Chinese residents of Manila.*

Manila flood, 1904

Dreaded Moro Pirates

An excerpt about pirates in the central Philippines from the book The Former Phillipines thru Foreign Eyes *by Tomas de Comyn and others, published in New York in 1917.*

Early in the morning I rode on the priest's horse to Legaspi, and in the evening through deep mud to the alcalde at Albay. We were now (June) in the middle of the so-called dry season, but it rained almost every day; and the road between Albay and Legaspi was worse than ever. During my visit information arrived from the commandant of the faluas on the south coast that, as he was pursuing two pirate vessels, six others suddenly made their appearance, in order to cut off his return; for which reason he had quickly made his way back. The faluas are very strongly manned, and provided with cannon, but the crews furnished by the localities on the coast are entirely unpractised in the use of fire-arms, and moreover hold the Moros in such dread that, if the smallest chance offers of flight,

they avail themselves of it to ensure their safety by making for the land. The places on the coast, destitute of other arms than wooden pikes, were completely exposed to the pirates, who had firmly established themselves in Catanduanes, Biri, and several small islands, and seized ships with impunity, or robbed men on the land. Almost daily fresh robberies and murders were announced from the villages on the shore. During a plundering expedition the men caught are employed at the oars and at its close sold as slaves; and, on the division of the spoil, one of the crew falls to the share of the dato (Moro chief) who fitted out the vessel.

Moro warriors, once the rulers of the central and southern :Philippines, in full battle gear. A photograph from around the year 1900

CAÑON REAL
FUNDICION DE
MANILA

Año
1655

Manila, in the 17th and 18th centuries, was the location of cannon foundries that were world famous. This is an image of a Manila cannon on a pirate ship in the Shanghai Disney resort. Of course, it is entirely possible that it is a copy, but it is, at least superficially, a good one.

Fearful Friars

An excerpt from Burton Holmes' travel narrative on Manila, published in 1908

Among the religious institutions the most imposing is the monastery of the Augustin friars. At the windows, white robed brethren now and then appear. The palatial pile adjoining it is Jesuit property. Its beautiful façade, apparently marble and mosaic, is in reality of wood, elaborately designed and painted in a most deceptive manner. We visited the interior of the Franciscan convento, where we were courteously welcomed by the friars. At the present moment, the long-robes, black and white and brown, once so conspicuous in the city streets, are rarely seen in public places. Though there are still several hundred monks houses in these many conventos, few dare to venture out. The Filipinos have too many old scores to settle. Occasionally, during concert hours when there is a reassuring number of our soldiers in evidence on the Luneta, a dozen friars may walk forth in groups for a sunset airing near the shore; but as a feature in the street life of Manila the friar is a reminiscence. It is not my province to discuss the influence for good or evil of these Spanish friars in the Philippines. Their rule is ended, and the church, at last awake to their shortcomings in the past, will, without doubt, under the guidance of American Catholics, transform the institutions which the friars have founded and fostered the Philippines into agencies for future good.

The old Bilibid prison, built in 1865 by the Spanish colonialists and photographed here in the 1870s.

Japanese Pirates etc.

A missive from the leading Catholic Church official in Manila, Geronimo de Alcaraz, to the king of Spain dated June 28, 1599. It lists the strategic challenges facing the Philippine venture:

The colony is surrounded by many and powerful heathen countries, who are hostile to the Christian faith. The insalubrious climate and various military expeditions are continually causing losses of men. Artillery and skilled workmen are greatly needed; and the fortifications need repair. The government of New Spain has given little attention to the needs of the Philippine colony. Japanese pirates have menaced Luzon, and the Chinese are suspected of plots against the Spaniards. Light sailing-vessels are being built for defense of the coast, since galleys cannot be used to advantage. Mindanao is pacified, but no tribute has yet been paid, and the country is poor. A rebellion in Cagayan has been put down, and the leaders executed; so that region is now pacified and secure. Dasmarinas's expedition to Camboja has proved a failure, and he is stranded on the Chinese coast, in great need; but Tello is unable to send him aid, and advises him to return to Manila. Aid for the poor soldiers is urgently needed and requested.

A Massacre of the Chinese

From The Former Philippines through Foreign Eyes *by Tomas de Comyn and others, published in 1917.*

In the attack of the noted pirate, Limahong, in 1574, they escaped destruction only by a miracle; and soon new dangers threatened them afresh. In 1603 a few mandarins came to Manila, under the pretence of ascertaining whether the ground about Cavite was really of gold. They were supposed to be spies, and it was concluded, from their peculiar mission, that an attack upon the colony was intended by the Chinese. The archbishop and the priests incited the distrust which was felt against the numerous Chinese who were settled in Manila. Mutual hate and suspicion arose; both parties feared one another and prepared for hostilities. The Chinese commenced the attack; but the united forces of the Spaniards, being supported by the Japanese and the Filipinos, twenty-three thousand, according to other reports twenty-five thousand, of the Chinese were either killed or driven into the desert. When the news of this massacre reached China, a letter from the Royal Commissioners was sent to the Governor

of Manila. The void occasioned by this massacre was soon filled up again by Chinese immigrants; and in 1662 the colony was once more menaced with a new and great danger, by the Chinese pirate Kog-seng, who had under his command between eighty and one hundred thousand men, and who already had dispossessed the Dutch of the Island of Formosa. He demanded the absolute submission of the Philippines; his sudden death, however, saved the colony, and occasioned a fresh outbreak of fury against the Chinese settlers in Manila, a great number of whom were butchered in their own "quarter." Some dispersed and hid themselves; a few in their terror plunged into the water or hanged themselves; and a great number fled in small boats to Formosa.

Within the Walls

Intramuros, which in Spanish means "within the walls," is the oldest district and the historic core of Manila. Districts beyond the walls were referred as the extramuros, "outside the walls." Construction of the walls was begun by Spanish colonial administration in the late 16th century to protect the city from foreign invasions, particularly pirate attacks. The walled area covered 0.67 square kilometres on the shore of Manila Bay, just south of the entrance to Pasig River. The fortifications include Fort Santiago. Intramuros was badly damaged during the battle to recapture the city from the Japanese in early 1945. Reconstruction of the walls started in 1951 and they are now a major tourist attraction.

> Intramuros! The old Manila. The original Manila. The Noble and Ever Loyal City ....To the early missionaries she was a new Rome, but to the early conquistadores, she was a new Solomon's Temple, filled with life and love, - but most of all with sound and music.
>
> *- Nick Joaquin*, Manila, My Manila, *1990*

Fort Santiago beside the Pasig, 1899

Sixty-Two Junks

From An Historical View of The Philippine Islands *by Martinez de Zuñiga, a translation of which was published in London in 1814.*

"Limahong was a pirate of such renown, that the Emperor of China had sent against him three different squadrons, and he was in fact so pressed on all sides by this force, that having captured a Chinese junk coming from Manila, who informed him of the new conquests by the Spaniards, he determined to sail for this country, and be crowned King of these islands, in order to be secure, by this means, from the Emperor's attacks. He arrived at the island of Corregidor, which is in the mouth of the bay, the 29th of November 1574, with sixty-two junks, in which he brought one thousand five hundred women, two thousand soldiers, and a great many seamen, sufficient artillery, muskets, and swords. The Spaniards had no intimation of his arrival at Corregidor, and the same night his second-in-command, who was a Japanese of the name of Sioco, landed with six hundred men, with which he entered, and attempted to take possession of Manila. In the attempt to land he lost three boats, which were swamped by the surf; but he effected his object, without being at all discovered by our people. He first landed at Parañaque, supposing it to be Manila, but soon finding out his mistake, he began his march to it by the beach, his vessels following him, and at day-break he arrived at Manila, where he was discovered by the Indians."

Fort Santiago

The fort, named after the patron saint of Spain, is part of the walled central area of Manila known as Intramuros. The first fort was a structure of palm logs and earth which was mostly destroyed when the city was attacked by Chinese pirates led by Lam Fung (sometimes known as Limahong) in 1574.

The original architect of Intramuros was a Spanish Jesuit priest named Antoñio Sedeño, work began in 1590 and was completed in 1593 during the administration of Governor-General Gomez Perez Dasmariñas.

Fort Santiago was long used as a detention center and worse by the Spanish. The reformist leader Jose Rizal was arrested by the Spanish and imprisoned in Fort Santiago, and was executed there by firing squad on December 30, 1896, less than two years before the collapse of Spanish power in the Philippines. The Japanese also used it as a prison and venue for torture, and around 600 American prisoners of war died in the Fort during the Japanese occupation 1942-45, mostly of suffocation and starvation.

Palace of the Governor

Built in 1599, the first Palacio del Gobernador (Palace of the Governor) was near Plaza de Armas in Fort Santiago. When the 1645 earthquake hit it was destroyed. The palace was the state residence of the Governor-General. After its destruction it was moved and reconstructed in 1733 and 1747. Tragedy struck again in 1771 when it was damaged by another earthquake. In 1850 a Spanish-type façade was added but was then destroyed by the earthquake of 1863. After all of this is was abandoned by the Governor-General who preferred to move his state residence to Malacañang.

Curfew

An excerpt from The Manila-Acapulco Galleons: The Treasure Ships of the Pacific *by Shirley Fish on how Filipinos were required by the Spaniards to interact with Chinese residents of Manila in the 17th century.*

If the Spaniards had allowed them to get on with their lives, they would have had a much better relationship with the Chinese, but their fears and biases sometimes led to ugly encounters including the revolts launched against them. However, as the Spaniards felt intimidated by the growing Chinese population of Manila, they decided to gather all of the Chinese who were living outside of the city walls, and segregate them into their own neighborhood which was known as the "Parian." From atop the city walls, armed soldiers monitored the activities of the Chinese in their community. They were free to roam around the entire city during the day, but in the evening hours there were expected to return to the Parian.

The Manila market, known as the Parian

A pontoon bridge erected across the Pasig River in 1863, after the bridge nearby, the Puente Grande, was badly damaged after a major earthquake. In the background is the Santo Domingo Church

The 1863 Earthquake

From The Former Philippines thru Foreign Eyes, *by Tomas de Comyn, and others, published in 1917.*

On June 3, 1863, at thirty-one minutes past seven in the evening, after a day of tremendous heat while all Manila was busy in its preparations for the festival of Corpus Christi, the ground suddenly rocked to and fro with great violence. The firmest buildings reeled visibly, walls crumbled, and beams snapped in two. The dreadful shock lasted half a minute; but this little interval was enough to change the whole town into a mass of ruins, and to bury alive hundreds of its inhabitants. A letter of the governor-general, which I have seen, states that the cathedral, the government-house, the barracks, and all the public buildings of Manila were entirely destroyed, and that the few private houses which remained standing threatened to fall in. Later accounts speak of four hundred killed and two thousand injured, and estimate the loss at eight millions of dollars. Forty-six public and five hundred and seventy private buildings were thrown down; twenty-eight public and five hundred twenty-eight private buildings were nearly destroyed, and all the houses left standing were more or less injured.

A view of the city of Manila in 1581 from Bagumbayan, now Rizal Park.

A painting of the Pasig River front in Manila in 1794, by the Italian painter Fernando Brambila.

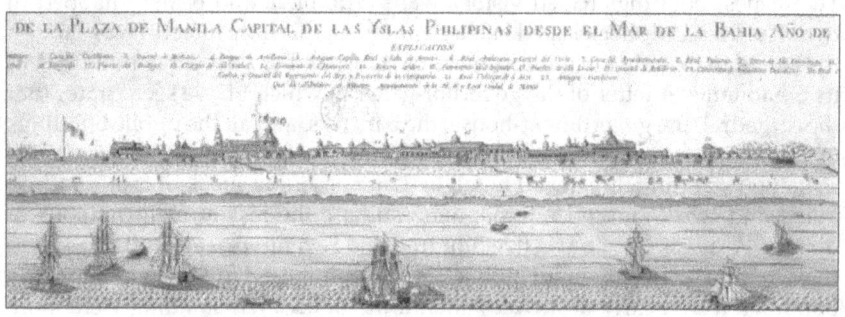

*An engraving from the year 1818, showing Manila Bay and the town,
by the artist Francisco Javier de Herrera.*

Shopping and Streets

Laurence Oliphant describes a street scene in Manila in 1857.

In obedience to the first and most natural impulse of a visitor to Manilla, we lost no time in making our way to the principal cheroot manufactory, and as we drove through the streets there was plenty to engage our attention. Their whole aspect, as well as that of the population with which they are crowded, differs entirely from that of any other town I had ever visited in the East. The houses are two-storied, the upper half forming the dwelling-house and the lower the shop. Bound the upper story runs a covered balcony, the sides and fronts composed of shutters divided into minute squares, which are filled with mother-of-pearl shells, the transparency of the nacre serving the purpose of glass. Beneath this balcony blue and white calico screens project, and fall beyond the side pavement in such a manner as to form a covered way for the passengers, sufficient not only to protect them from the sun, but to conceal them from the view of any body in the centre of the street. These screens are put up in accordance with a municipal regulation, and when they are new, and the colors are fresh, give a gay appearance to the streets.

A painting representing the Philippine Revolution by Carlos "Botong" Francisco (1912-1969)

Plaza Mayor, Intramuros

Northwest Airlines advert

Newsclipping from The Scranton Republican Nov 4, 1906

The San Miguel Brewery in the early 1900s.

Wet Your Whistle

Probably the best-known Filipino brand around the world is the beer San Miguel. The San Miguel Brewery was founded in 1890 and advertised itself as "The brewery that brews beer to suit the climate." Today, San Miguel has 95% market share in the Philippines.

San Miguel label

The loading bay at the back of the old San Miguel Brewery

Cigars

Philippine cigars are probably the most famous in the world, after Cuban cigars, and the connection is climate and the Spanish empire. The Spanish started planting tobacco in the Philippines in the late 1500s, and the plant prospered, and so did the businesses that sold it. The Filipinos quickly took to smoking tobacco, and it became a national pastime. The Spanish made the industry a monopoly in the 17th century, and it remains highly regulated.

Tobacoo adverts and labels

Tobacoo labels

Filipino-children-smoking

A Cosmopolitan Crowd

Laurence Oliphant, visiting Manila in 1857, describes the hotel he stayed at and the amazing range of people he found there.

In ascending the river, the fortified town, containing the garrison and residences of the officials, is on the right-hand side; on the other is a densely populated suburb, in which the shops, hotels, and foreigners' houses are situated. This is intersected by sundry canals running at right angles to the river, crowded with boats, and on the banks of one of these stood the hotel to which we were destined. It was patronized by what Americans would call "a mixed crowd," chiefly captains of merchantmen from every quarter of the globe, but whose polyglot conversation did not at all perplex our bustling hostess, as she spoke, during breakfast, English, French, Spanish, Malay, and Hindostanee, all with such perfect fluency that her own nationality remained a mystery.

41

Chinatown 1949

Along Escolta street in 1899

Getting Around in Old Manila

The tranvia was the first public transit system in Manila, established in 1882, the precursor of today's LRT. The company was called the La Compañia de Tranvias de Filipinas, owned by Leon Monssour. It operated five routes, four of them with horse-drawn carriages and one line, the Malabon line, using a steam engine to pull the carriages along the track.

The steam-powered tranvia operated until 1898, and the tranvia was a key form of transport in Manila until 1902, when the company operating it ran into problems. In that year, the city authorities decided to build an electric power station and power network, and the result was the creation of Meralco, originally called Manila Electric Railroad and Light Company.

The company took over the transport routes operated by La Compañia de Tranvias de Filipinas and by 1913 had nine electric tram routes in operation.

The steam-powered Travia pictured in 1883

The Caraboa

A description of the caraboa, the local word for water buffalo, from travel writer Burton Holmes, published in 1908. The front he refers to was the battle between the invading US forces and the remnants of the Philippine independence movement.

A curious feature of the street life of Manila is the carabao, or water buffalo, a creature slow, deliberate, and dignified, scores of which pass our dwelling every day, dragging in their lazy wake long trains of carts now used for forwarding supplies to soldiers at the front; all night we hear the laden cart go creaking by.

carabao-cart

Spanish Governor-Generals office, 1899

Moats

An excerpt from Manila, The Burton Holmes Travelogues *in the early 1900s.*

The medieval moats of Old Manila are very picturesque; we skirt them every day in driving to and from Escolta. Manila's medieval walls were once models for defenses of their kind. They were reared more than three hundred years ago. Beyond them rises the long roof of a monastery, one of the many somber piles raised by Spanish friars in this Oriental stronghold of Catholicism.

Image of the moat and wall of Fort Santiago

The Governors

From 1565 to the 20th century, the Philippines was rules by over a hundred different men, most of them with the title of Governor-General in the name of the King of Spain.

The first Spanish governor was Miguel Lopez de Legazpi (1565-1572), who chose Manila as the seat of government. The 46th governor, also at the time the senior Catholic official in Manila, Archbishop Manuel Rojo del Rio y Vieyra, was forced to hand over power to the British on October 6, 1762. The British appointed two governors before handing it back to the Spanish after the Treaty was signed, ending the Seven Years War.

Between 1762 and 1899 when Spanish rule in the Philippines ended, a further 130 men, one after the other, served as governor. One of them - Simón de Anda y Salazar - had also been one of the two British governors.

Then in 1899 came the Americans, and 35 men held power in succession, up to 1941, including future US president William Taft, and Theodore Roosevelt III, son of President Theodore Roosevelt.

During the Japanese occupation 1941-1945, four military men held the job of governor of the Philippines. The Americans returned in 1945 and the following year, on July 4, 1946, the last US High Commissioner, Paul McNutt, became the US ambassador to the Philippines and the era of foreign governors was over.

The first Governor-General, Miguel Lopez de Legazpi (1565-1572).

Archbishop Manuel Rojo del Rio y Vieyra, the 46th Governor General (1761-1762)

Wesley Merritt (Aug 14, 1898- Aug 30, 1898)

Elwell S. Otis (Aug 28, 1898- May 5, 1900)

Arthur MacArthur, Jr (May 5, 1900 - July 4, 1901)

Adna Chaffee (July 4, 1901 July 4, 1902)

Manila's Oldest Restaurant

Ambon Mundos claims to be the oldest restaurant in the city. Founded in 1888, its name means "Both worlds", and its menu offers both Spanish and Filipino dishes. The Paella Manilena is highly recommended.

mundos

Like All Spanish Towns

An excerpt from My Mother's Journal; a young lady's diary of five years spent in Manila, Macao, and the Cape of Good Hope from 1829-1834, *by Harriet Hillard and Katharine Hillard, published in 1900.*

I really do not know what to say about Manila. You cannot get any idea of it from description. I am told it is like all Spanish towns, the forts, convents and churches taking up a large part of the place. The roofs of the houses are covered with tiles. They are mostly of one story only, and some are very spacious. They have no glass windows; but they are made of pearl-shell in little squares, and some of them have Venetian blinds. The houses are all whitewashed, but are soon turned black by the climate, which gives the whole city the appearance of having been smoked, as by a great fire. An immense number of people live on the water in boats.

The Commercial Gene

Laurence Oliphant, visiting Manila in 1857, talks about the different approach of Chinese and Filipino shopkeepers to the prospect of business.

Shopping at Manilla is an unsatisfactory pursuit. The principal streets are the Escolta and Rosario; but all the best shops are kept by Chinamen, who fairly beat the mestizoes out of the field as traders. The superior industry, intelligence, and economical habits of the pure Chinaman give him an immense advantage over the mestizo. The former despises feast-days, and cares little for personal comfort; he lives in the little shop which contains his stock in trade, and keeps his eyes open. The mestizo spends half his existence in a gala dress, does not condescend to live in his shop, and has no business habits when he is there. In the middle of the day he is generally asleep, and is excessively disgusted at being roused to serve a customer. It is not at all an uncommon thing to see a man coiled up snoring in one corner of his shop, and a mestizo girl stretched luxuriously at full length upon the counter, her beautiful black hair thrown back from her face, falling in wavy massive folds to the ground, and her bosom heaving so softly and regularly with the long-drawn breath of a profound slumber, that, rather than do violence to his aesthetic nature by disturbing sleeping beauty, the purchaser moves gently on to the next shop, and finds a grinning Chinaman, with his eyes so destitute of lids that he looks as if he could not wink, much less sleep, but which sparkle with intelligence and cupidity, who is imbued with the firm determination, if he does not possess in his shop the article which you do want, to force you to buy from him something you do not.

The original and largest pharmacy in the Philippines, Botica Boie

The World's Oldest Chinatown

Binondo, known as the world's oldest Chinatown, was established in 1594 by the Spanish as the designated settlement for Catholic Chinese in Manila. It is located across the Pasig River from Intramuros, from where the colonial rulers could keep an eye on things.

From The Former Philippines thru Foreign Eyes, *by Tomas de Comyn etc, 1917.*

The suburbs, or Binondo quarter, contain more inhabitants than the city itself, and is the commercial town. They have all the stir and life incident to a large population actively engaged in trade, and in this respect the contrast with the city proper is great.

From Recollections of Manila and the Philippines During 1848, 1849 and 1850.

The great object of the Chinese shopmen appears to be to show the most varied, and frequently miscellaneous, collection of goods in the smallest possible space; as, their shops being for the most part not more than ten feet broad towards the street, leaves but little space besides the doorway to display the attractions.

Manila's Chinatown in the 1920s

Chinese and Mestizos

From Recollections of Manila and the Philippines During 1848, 1849 and 1850 *by Robert Mac Micking.*

The great object of the Chinese shopmen appears to be to show the most varied, and frequently miscellaneous, collection of goods in the smallest possible space; as, their shops being for the most part not more than ten feet broad towards the street, leaves but little space besides the doorway to display the attractions of their wares, and every inch has to be made the most of by them. These China shopkeepers have nearly driven all competition, except with each other out of the market, — very few Mestizos or Spaniards being able to live on the small profits which the competition among themselves has reduced them to. A China shopkeeper generally makes his shop his home, all of them sleeping in those confined dens at night, from which, on opening their doors about five in the morning, as they usually do, a most noisome and pestiferous smell issues and is diffused through the streets. The Mestizos cannot do this, but must have a house to live in out of the profits of the shop; and the consequence has been, that when their shopkeeping profits could no longer do that, they have nearly all betaken themselves to other more suitable occupations, from which the energies of their Chinese rivals are less likely to drive them. The number of Chinamen in Manila and throughout the islands is very great, and nearly the whole provincial trade in manufactured goods is in their hands.

Murder and a Sunset

An excerpt from an article headlined "Beautiful Manila Bay Sunset hides Unbelievable Ugliness and Squalor", written by Arnold Dibble and published in the Brownsville Herald *in 1969.*

MANILA - The sunset on Manila Bay is one of the most beautiful sights in the world. But the same sun also sets over city squalor and ugliness so revolting as to be almost unbelievable.Manila lives for its sunsets, the kind you question on airline calendars as too beautiful to be true. But each day between those sunsets an average of at least three persons in the city die violently. This is a city of incredible beauty - and of incredible violence and meanness.

Public Bathing Along the Pasig River

From A History and Description of Our Philippine Wonderland, *by Adjutant E. Hannaford, published in 1899, just after the Americans occupied the Philippines.*

"Toward the evening parties of bathers, people of all ages and both sexes, multiply along the bank, or are already splashing about in the water with lighthearted glee. Great water-buffaloes with wide-spreading horns come singly or several together for the bath that rewards their afternoon toil in the fields or on the road."

Public bathing in the Pasig River. Around the year 1900

Binondo Church Manila 1899

The Carabao and the Shell

A Filipino Folktale about a water buffalo and a mollusc.

On a very hot day, when a carabao went into the river to bathe, he met a shell and they began talking.

"You are very slow," said the carabao to the shell.

"Oh, no," replied the shell. "I can beat you in a race."

"Then let us try and see," said the carabao.

So they went out on the bank and the carabao started to run. After he had gone a distance, he stopped and called, "Shell!"

And another shell lying by the river answered, "Here I am!"

The carabao, thinking that it was the same shell with which he was racing, ran on.

By and by he stopped again and called, "Shell!" And another shell answered, "Here I am!"

The carabao was surprised that the shell could keep up with him. But he ran on and on, and every time he stopped to call, another shell answered him. But he was determined that the shell should not beat him, so he ran until he dropped dead.

An image of indigenous tribesmen armed with knives, taken around the year 1900

53

A Hardy Church

San Agustin Church in Manila is one of four churches constructed during the Spanish colonial era that has been designated by UNESCO as a World Heritage Site. The present structure is in fact the third church to be built on the site. The first was made of bamboo in 1571, soon after the Spanish arrived, and burned down three years later during a pirate attack. A second church made of wood was also destroyed in a fire in 1583 when a candle set fire to the drapes of the funeral bier of the Spanish Governor-General Gonzalo Ronquillo de Peñalosa. Third time lucky and following precisely the story of the three little pigs, the Augustin monks next built a stone church, completed in 1604. The

San Agustin Church post-earthquake

The church survived many earthquakes unscathed, but was badly damaged in an earthquake in 1880, as a result of which one of the two towers was demolished. The church was the place where the terms for the handover of power from the Spanish to the Americans in 1898 were worked out. During the Japanese occupation of Manila 1942-45, the church was used as an internment center for enemy aliens, and many of the inmates died, particularly in the fierce fighting preceding the Japanese surrender in May 1945. But it was the only one of seven churches in the Intramuros to remain standing after the war.

A used car dealer in Manila in the 1930s

A Higher Education

The University of Santo Tomas (UST) is the oldest university in Asia, and is the largest Catholic university in the world in terms of student population on a single campus. It was set up by Bishop Miguel de Benavides, the third Archbishop of Manila as a seminary to prepare young Filipino men for the priesthood, and it opened on April 28, 1611. In 1645, Pope Innocent X upgraded the college to a university and in 1680, the Spanish king became its patron.

Santo Tomas assembly room 1887

Santo Tomas library 1887

University of Santo Tomas

Félix Resurrección Hidalgo

Félix Resurrección Hidalgo y Padilla was born in 1855 and became the most famous Filipino artist of his era. He was involved with many of the members of the Philippine reform movement who opposed both the Spanish and American colonial administrations. He died in 1913, and one of Manila's main thoroughfares was named after him.

The Manila Earnshaws

Tomas Gavino Noguera Earnshaw was born in 1867 in Cavites near Manila and was the mayor of Manila from 1927 to 1933. He died in 1954. His elder brother Manuel Earnshaw, born in 1862, served as Resident Commissioner in the Philippines from 1913 to 1917, during the American administration. Tomas was a naval engineer, industrialist and public servant. He was a co-founder of Manuel Earnshaw & Company and Earnshaw Shipways and Engineering Company. How the Earnshaw name, also on this book, made its way to the Philippines is not clear.

Manila street at the end of the 19th century, with a tram and many horse-drawn carriages

Two Horses Liberated

From Manila, The Burton Holmes Travelogues *by Burton Holmes. McClure 1908*

In Spanish days the tram-cars, invariably crowded, were drawn by a single miserable pony; but our people decided that such a system should not flourish in the shadow of our humanizing institutions.The governor accordingly compelled the English tram-way company to hitch two ponies to each car. Even the pair proved inadequate, whereupon the people took a hand, as witnessed by an incident, which is, I think, unique in the history of city railway companies. On the Fourth of July a crowded car was on its way to the Luneta. The two little brutes attached could barely crawl, one of them was upon the point of dropping from exhaustion. The passengers, among them many soldiers, held a brief consultation, and decided on a course of action. They turned the two poor creatures loose in the neglected Botanical Garden, and put shoulders to the horseless car, and pushed it with its load of women and children and a few lazy men to the scene of the celebration, three quarters of a mile away.

How to Describe Manila?

Miguel Syjuco is a Filipino writer born in Manila in 1976 who won the 2008 Man Asian Literary Prize for his first novel Ilustrado.

"You can't bring an unwritten place to life without losing something substantial. Manila is the cradle, the graveyard, the memory. The Mecca, the Cathedral, the bordello. The shopping mall, the urinal, the discotheque. I'm hardly speaking in metaphor. It's the most impermeable of cities. How does one convey all that?"

Puente de España

Through history, there was have been two main bridges linking the center of Manila, Intramuros, with Binondo on the other side of the Pasig River. The first was the Puente Grande (The Great Bridge), made of wood and completed in 1630. It was rebuilt in stone in 1814 and renamed Puente de Piedra (The Stone Bridge), but was badly damaged in the earthquake of 1863, and was repaired and renamed Puente de España (The Bridge of Spain). Disaster struck again during a typhoon in 1914, and the idle section of the bridge was lost. The Americans in charge of Manila decided to construct a new bridge nearby, called Jones Bridge (Puente Jones), and Puente de Espana was dismantled.

The Bridge of Spain, across the Pasig River, shown in a postcard from around 1900

An Epidemic Leads to a Massacre

A cholera epidemic hit Manila in 1820, part of a pandemic that hit many parts of Asia that year, and many died. But the worst part of the story is the crazed murders that accompanied the epidemic. The first cholera case was found on October 4, and some of the local people decided that the disease had been brought in by foreigners who had poisoned the river. The panic focused on the French, who were believed to want to take the country from the Spanish, and that killing the natives with disease was part of the plan. A mob formed on October 9 and attacked non-Spanish foreigners. Among the eyewitnesses was Pierre Dobell, an American who served as the Imperial Russian Consul in Manila. He said many of the victims were "so cut up and mangled that it was impossible to recognize them." More than twenty Europeans and several Chinese died at the hands of the mob.

An illustration from the book "Twenty Years in the Philippines (1819-1839)" by Paul de la Gironiere. Showing an altercation during the 1820 cholera epidemic in Manila

Yo-Yo Hunting

When the Spanish arrived in the Philippines in the 16th century, they observed that one hunting trick the tribespeople in the mountain areas of Luzon used was to hide in trees and use a rock tied to a long piece of string which they threw at wild animals that passed beneath them. The string allowed them to retrieve the rock and throw it it again. Some say this is the derivation of the yo-yo, but it probably wasn't. It appears the toy was invented in China, and variations of it were known in Europe centuries ago. But the modern yo-yo definitely has a Philippine angle to it. It was described in an issue of Scientific American magazine in 1916 as being a "Filipino Toy", and a Filipino named Pedro Flores took a yo-yo to the United States in 1928 and set up a company there to produce them. The name comes from the indigenous Ilocano language and is said to mean "come back". A businessman named Donald Duncan saw Flores playing with the yo-yo in San Francisco in the late 1920s, realized its potential and bought out Flores' company. By the late 1940s, the Duncan company was producing millions of yo-yos, made of wood, every year. In the 1960s, plastic yo-yos appeared, and Duncan lost control of the patent and of the market and went into bankruptcy. But the yo-yo lives on.

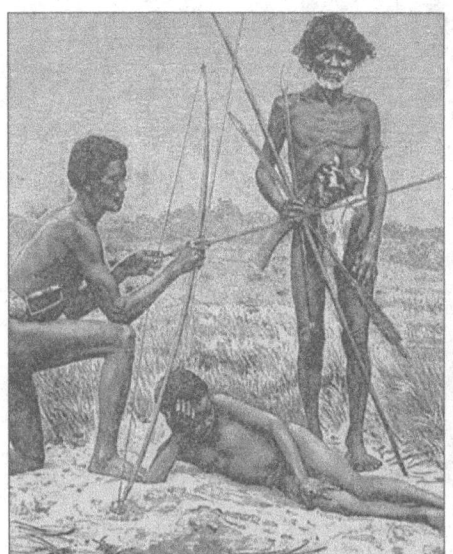 

Images from the 19th century showing the weaponry used by Philippine tribespeople.

Bibles and Revolvers

Laurence Oliphant was accompanying the British envoy Lord Elgin on his trip to China in 1857 when he had the chance to do a side trip to Manila. Here is an excerpt talking about the scene when his ship, the British man-of-war HMS Furious, docked at the wharf in the town.

Small river boats, full of vegetables or passengers, cut in and out; groups of women are collected on the steps bathing; and Custom-house guards lounge upon the river brink, but they have a proper respect for a British man-of-war's gig, and allow us to reach our landing place unchallenged, and carry our portmanteaus to the hotel without manifesting the slightest curiosity to know whether they contain the two articles which are perhaps most commonly to be found in every traveler's luggage, but which are most strictly prohibited from being landed at Manilla, to wit, Bibles and revolvers.

The official Coat of Arms of the City of Manila, granted by the Spanish king in 1596.

The official Coat of Arms of the City of Manila today, a modification of the colonial design.

Salambaw

The Salambaw was a fishing implement, a huge net fixed in a frame with usually four arms that was lowered into the water, then lifted back after a time. It was common along the Philippine coast and also found in some places in southern China. In El Filibusterismo, the writer, revolutionary national martyr Jose Rizal described the salambaw as an "insecure fishing apparatus which in their movements resemble skeletons of giants saluting an antediluvian tortoise."

Salambaw fishing nets on vast bamboo frames. The lower images also show the Pasig River lighthouse.

Speed Limits for Water Buffalo

An excerpt from Interesting Manila, *by George Miller, published in 1906 about a unique problem on Manila streets in that era.*

The Oriental citizen is so peaceful that there is rarely anything so lively as a good street row, but once in a while something does happen that is worth while. There is a tradition carefully preserved (in alcohol?) that on one occasion just after the civil government took charge of affairs and before Br'er Taft had got the situation well in hand, a carabao ran away on the Escolta. The excitement was tremendous. A crowd gathered, and some of the imaginative ones averred that they could actually see the animal move without taking micrometer measurement. So rapid was the transit that a man, who was eating his lunch at Clarke's, found that, during the time he spent at the table, the runaway had passed the building. The native policemen were helpless in the face of emergency, and an American patrolman was summoned, who with great presence of mind approached the carreton, wakened the sleeping driver, informed him that his carabao was running away, and assisted in restoring order generally. The commission at once passed an act regulating the speed of carabaos within city limits, which has been faithfully maintained ever since.

Manila Bay in 1826, a painting by the Russian adventurer Louis Choric

Lottery-Row

The following is an excerpt from Rudyard Kipling's poem *The Lost Legions*, published in 1895, in honor, one presumes, of the many anonymous soldiers of fortune and adventurers who helped extend the British Empire. It lists out many parts of the world that would have been well-known to his readers at the time. The phrase "An I.D.B. race on the Pan" refers to diamond smuggling in South Africa. I.D.B. stood for "Illicit Diamond Buyers", the race was to escape the police and the Pan was Du Toit's Pan in Kimberley. The Lottery row in Manila is less clear, though a guess would be gambling dens.

> The ends o' the Earth were our portion,
> The ocean at large was our share.
> There was never a skirmish to windward
> But the Leaderless Legion was there:
> Yes, somehow and somewhere and always
> We were first when the trouble began,
> From a lottery-row in Manila,
> To an I.D.B. race on the Pan
> (Dear boys!),
> With the Mounted Police on the Pan.

A depiction of the fighting in 1899 between the Philippine Republic forces and the invading Americans

The Terraces of the Cordilleras

The Banaue Rice Terraces were constructed in the mountains of Ifugao in the north of Luzon Island starting around 2,000 years ago. Terraced rice culture has been central to the lives of the Ifugao people ever since. The terraces are made of stone and mud and intricately trace the contours of the Cordillera Mountains. They are fed by an irrigation system from the rainforests above the terraces. They were designated a UNESCO World Heritage site in 1995.

No Inheritance

From R.F. Barton, published in 1919 by the University of California Press.

Family properties consist of rice lands, forest lands and heirlooms. The Ifugao attitude is that lands and articles of value that have been handed down from generation to generation cannot be the property of any individual. Present holders possess only a transient and fleeting possession, or better, occupation, insignificant in duration in comparison with the decades and perhaps centuries that have usually elapsed since the field or heirloom came into the possession of the family.

National Martyr, José Rizal

José Rizal was born on June 19, 1861, in Calamba, a town south of Manila. He was a brilliant student and quickly became proficient in multiple languages. He studied medicine in Manila, and went to Spain in 1882 to complete his degree. While in Europe he wrote critically about Spain's colonial rule of the Philippines, and joined in the Propaganda Movement which included other Filipinos pushing for reform. He wrote a novel, *Noli Me Tangere* (Touch Me Not), a work that describes the dark aspects of Spain's colonial rule, focusing on the role of Catholic priests. The book was banned in the Philippines.

Rizal returned to the Philippines in 1887, but he immediately left when he was targeted by the Spanish police as a result of his novel, but moved back in 1892 because he felt he needed to be in the country to play

José Rizal

a role in change. The reform society he founded, the Liga Filipino (Philippine League), was banned and Rizal was exiled to Dapitan, in Mindanao for four years during which time he practiced medicine.

In 1895, Rizal asked for permission to travel to Cuba as an army doctor. His request was approved, but in August 1896 there was a revolt led by Katipunan, a nationalist Filipino society founded by Andres Bonifacio. Rival had no ties to the group and disapproved of its violent approach, but he was arrested and after a show trial, was convicted of sedition and sentenced to death by firing squad.

Rizal, then 35 years old, was publically executed in Manila on December 30, 1896. His last words were "Consummatum Est!" (It is finished). Two years later, the Spanish were gone. Rizal remains a nationalist icon in the Philippines.

Rizal the Cartoonist

José Rizal is regarded as the "Father of Philippine Comics" because of a number of illustrations he drew while in Germany.

The drawings, entitled "The baptism of two brothers", were inspired by the German cartoon "Max and Moritz" and were created by Rizal to entertain the children of his landlord, Pastor Ulmer. The original drawing is in the National Library of the Philippines, in Manila.

A Letter to Say Goodbye

Jose Rizal, the reformer executed by the Spanish on December 30, 1896, wrote the following letter to his brother the night before he died.

My dear Brother,

When you receive this letter, I shall be dead by then. Tomorrow at seven, I shall be shot; but I am innocent of the crime of rebellion. I am going to die with a tranquil conscience.

Adieu, my best, my dearest friend, and never think ill of me!

José Rizal

Fort Santiago,

29 December 1896

Regards to the whole family, to Sra. Rosa, Lolena, Conradito, and Federico. I leave a book for you as my remembrance

> One only dies once, and if one does not die well, a good opportunity is lost and will nor present itself again.
>
> Jose Rizal

The Philippine Flag

The Philippine flag was first sewn together by revolutionaries in hiding in Hong Kong. It was first seen in public during an armed clash May 28, 1898 and was formally unfurled by President Emilio Aguinaldo during the proclamation of Philippine independence on June 12, 1898. The symbolic significance of the flag is explained in the Proclamation of Philippine Independence, given below. The first version, interestingly, assumed that the United States would support the new republic, but they did not.

Misplaced Trust

Part of the Proclamation of Philippine Independence, August 1, 1898, referring to the national flag design.

"...And, lastly, it was resolved unanimously that this Nation, already free and independent as of this day, must use the same flag which up to now is being used, whose design and colors are found described in the attached drawing, the white triangle signifying the distinctive emblem of the famous Society of the Katipunan, which by means of its blood-compact inspired the masses to rise in revolution; the three stars, signifying the three principal islands of this Archipelago - Luzon, Mindanao and Panay where this revolutionary movement started; the sun representing the gigantic steps made by the sons of the country along the path of Progress and Civilization; the eight rays, signifying the eight provinces -Manila, Cavite, Bulacan, Pampanga, Nueva Ecija, Bataan, Laguna and Batangas - which declared themselves in a state of war as soon as the first revolt was initiated; and the colors of Blue, Red and White, commemorating the flag of the United States of North America, as a manifestation of our profound gratitude towards this Great Nation for its disinterested protection which it lent us and continues lending us."

The KKK

The Katipunan (KKK) was a Philippine revolutionary society founded by anti-Spanish Filipinos in 1892. Their goal was to gain independence from Spain. Its official name was Samahang Kataastaasan, Kagalanggalang Katipunan nh mga Anak ng Bayan (Supreme and Most Honorable Society of the Children of the Nation). It was founded by Andrés Bonifacio, Ladislao Diwa, and Teodoro Plata on the night that José Rizal was banished from the Philippines. They succeeded in establishing the first Philippine Republic, a short-lived entity proclaimed in January 23, 1899. The United States then invaded, took over the Philippines and wiped out any remaining vestiges of the KKK.

Irrational Chaos

Alex Garland, sums up the Philippines in his novel The Beach, *published in 1996.*
"I knew my affection for the Philippines was equally as telling: a democracy on paper, apparently well ordered, regularly subverted by irrational chaos. A place where I'd felt instantly at home."

The Mother of the Revolution

Melchora Aquino was born in 1812, gave birth to six children and in her eighties provided support and shelter to the young revolutionaries who were trying to kick the Spaniards out of the Philippines. The start of the revolution was declared in 1896 in her house. She was deported by the Spanish to Guam, and returned after the Americans took over the country. She died in 1919 at the age of 107.

Melchora Aquino, mother of the Philippine revolution. She lived to 107

Room 22

The Hotel de Oriente was said to be the first luxury hotel in the Philippines. It was constructed in the bustling commercial district of Binondo in Manila, just across the Pasig River from Intramuros, the center of the Spanish administration. Binondo had been established in the 16th century by the Spanish as a Chinatown, the first in the world: the Chinese in Manila were required to live there. The Hotel de Oriente opened in 1889, and had three floors and a total of 83 rooms, equipped with ceiling fans and electricity. It was located next to La Insular Cigar and Cigarette Factory, a crucial business for the economy. After the American takeover of the Philippines in 1899 following the Spanish-American War, the hotel was put to various official purposes, but was destroyed in World War II, during the Japanese occupation. The hotel's other claim to fame is that the revolutionary hero Jose Rizal, then working for independence of the Philippines from the Spanish, stayed there in 1892, in Room 22.

The Hotel de Oriente, Manila's first luxury hotel

The First Filipino Saint

Lorenzo Ruiz was born in the year 1600 in Manila's Chinatown, an area across the river designated specifically for Chinese Catholics. His father was Chinese and his mother Filipina, and he grew up as an altar boy in the Binondo Church, which is still standing. In 1636, he was accused of killing a Spaniard and escaped from Manila on a ship with Dominican monks heading for Japan. The rulers of Japan at the time, the Tokugawa Shogunate, had just started persecuting Christians, aiming to wipe out the religion on their turf, and the monks and Ruiz were all arrested and tortured to make them renounce their religion. On 27 September 1637, Ruiz was taken to the Nishizaka Hill, and hung upside down over a pit with one hand unbound so that he could signal his decision to recant, but he didn't.

An illustration from the 17th century showing how Christian martyrs were tortured to death in Japan

Ruiz was beatified by Pope John Paul II in 1981 on his visit to Manila, and his sainthood was formalized in 1987. Saint Lorenzo Ruiz de Manila is now the patron saint of the Philippines and of the Philippine people.

A Thousand Lives

The last words of Lorenzo Ruiz before he died in Nagasaki, Japan in 1637, executed by torture because he refused to recant his Christian faith. He spoke, it is believed, in Latin:

"Ego Catholicus sum et animo prompto paratoque pro Deo mortem obibo.

Si mille vitas haberem, cunctas ei offerrem."

("I am a Catholic and wholeheartedly do accept death for God; Had I a thousand lives, all these to Him shall I offer.")

The
American
Era

The Battle of Manila 1898

Telegrams sent between Secretary of the Navy John Long and Commodore Dewey on the order for and the result of the attack by A meridian forces on the Spanish forces in the Philippines.

Secretary of the Navy to Commodore Dewey Washington, April 24th
"Dewey, Hong Kong, China: War has commenced between Spain and the United States. Proceed at once to Philippine Islands. Commence operations at once, particularly against the Spanish fleet. You must capture vessels or destroy them. Use utmost endeavours."

Commodore Dewey to the Secretary of the Navy. Manila, May 1st
"The squadron arrived at Manila at daybreak this morning. Immediately engaged the enemy and destroyed the following Spanish vessels: "Reina Cristina," "Castilla Ulloa," "Isla de Cuba," "Isla de Luzon," "General Lezo," "Duero," "Correo," "Velasco," transport "Mindanao," and water battery at Cavite. The squadron is uninjured and only a few men slightly injured. The only means of telegraphing is to the American Consul in Hong Kong. I shall communicate with him."

Dewey, Cavite, May 4th
"I have taken possession of Naval Station at Cavite, on Philippine Islands. Have destroyed the fortifications at bay entrance, paroling garrison. I control bay completely and can take city at any time. The

MANILA FALLS.

Augustin Flees to Hong Kong in a German Vessel.

Washington, Aug. 15.—The Department of State has just issued the following:

The following dispatch was received at the Department of State at 11.15 P. M., August 15th, from Consul Wildman, Hong Kong: "Augustin says Dewey bombarded Manila Saturday, city surrendered unconditionally. Augustin was taken by Germans in launch to "Kaiserin Augustin" and brought to Hong Kong. I credit report.

DEWEY GAVE THEM ONE HOUR.

When the Spaniards Refused to Surrender He Opened Fire.

THE WHITE FLAG WENT UP

Governor Augustin Taken Off by a German Warship.

LITTLE DAMAGE TO MANILA

squadron is in excellent health and spirits. Spanish loss not fully known, but very heavy. 150 killed, including Captain on "Reina Cristina." I am assisting in protecting Spanish sick and wounded. 256 wounded in hospitals within our lines. Much excitement in Manila. Will protect foreign residents.

Telegram from Secretary Long to Commodore Dewey. May 7th
"Dewey, care American Consul, Hong Kong. The President, in the name of the American people, thanks you and your officers and men for your splendid achievement and overwhelming victory. In recognition, he has appointed you Rear Admiral, and will recommend a vote of thanks to you by Congress as a foundation for further promotion."

The Battle of Manila on May 1, 1898 was in many ways the start of the "American century". The US fleet destroyed the Spanish Pacific Fleet with the loss of no men, and only 19 injured.

The Battle of Manila so captured the US popular imagination that it was made into a board game

I have heard it said that life in Manila is extremely monotonous; but, during my stay, it seemed to me full of interest and animation.
- *Sir John Bowring, Governor of Hong Kong,*
after a visit to Manila in 1860.

The Philippine-American War

With the defeat of the Spanish forces, many Filipinos thought the Americans would support Philippine independence. This was not to be, and the result was a three-year war, 1899 to 1902 against the American occupation. The last remnants of the independence forces were only defeated in 1913. The impact of the war was such that the US laid out a roadmap to independence which was to end in 1944. The Japanese invasion intervened, but the Philippines became independent in 1946.

1898 May US Newspaper, 18981

Freedom Won the Day

Horace Spencer Fiske was an American writer and academic who wrote a poem in the classical style celebrating the Battle of Manila Bay and praising Commodore Dewey to well beyond the skies. The poem is long and begins and ends with this stanza:

And men by a million hearth-fires shall tell of Manila Bay
How Dewey swept past the forts at night,
And struck the Dons in the flushing light,
And for freedom won the day.

Fisk, fully in tune with the high-tech of the times, opens the story with Dewey and his fleet anchored off Hong Kong, and receiving the order to attack from Washington via an undersea telegraph cable:

In Hongkong harbor, far away, beyond the Philippines,
The "Acting Admiral" held his ships, no stauncher sea-machines;
And the 'jackies" grumbled and fumed and swore at the government's slow delay,
When the enemy lay so very near in the fair Manila Bay.
Till the President spoke beneath the waves-e'en hail the world around
And the Commodore caught with eager ear the deep electric sound.

The penultimate stanza, includes these lines:

And over the crumbling Spanish forts and the island by the sea
Instead of the Spaniards' jaundiced flag the Stars and Stripes flew free ...

A medal was struck by the US government to celebrate the victory in Manila Bay, which featured Commodore Dewey's portrait and the words "Hero of Manila".

You must capture vessels or destroy them. Use utmost endeavors.
– *President McKinley to Commodore George Dewey before the Battle of Manila in 1898. Dewey decimated the Spanish fleet and the Americans took the Philippines*

Trusting America

From The Good Fight *by Manuel Luis Quezon, published in 1946*

"From the grandstand, I went through streets crowded with people acclaiming their first president, on to the palace of Malacanan, the great mansion on the bank of the Pasig River which had been the seat of power for foreign rulers for many decades past. As I stepped out of the presidential car and walked over the marble floor of the entrance hall, and up the wide stairway, I remembered the legend of the mother of Rizal, the great Filipino martyr and hero, who went up those stairs on her knees to seek executive clemency from the cruel Spanish Governor-General Polavieja, that would save her son's life. This story has something to do with my reluctance to believe that capital punishment should ever be carried out. As a matter of fact, during my presidency no man ever went to the electric chair. At the last moment I always stayed the hand of the executioner. From the top of the stairs, turning to the right, one saw the very large reception hall, at the end of which on either side of the hall and fronting each other, there were two rooms which reminded me of my first visit to the palace. In the room on the right side of the hall, there stood at the time General Arthur MacArthur, then Military Governor of the Philippines, and on the left there was the room where Aguinaldo was kept a prisoner of war. The first thought that came to me was that I had been right in placing my faith in America, for by cooperating with her my people had won their local autonomy and were on the road to complete independence."

Malacanang Presidential Palace

The White Man's Burden

In February 1899, British writer and poet Rudyard Kipling wrote a poem entitled "The White Man's Burden: The United States and The Philippine Islands." Kipling was urging the U.S. to take up the "burden" of empire, as had Britain and other European nations.

Take up the White Man's burden
Send forth the best ye breed
Go send your sons to exile
To serve your captives' need
To wait in heavy harness
On fluttered folk and wild
Your new-caught, sullen peoples,
Half devil and half child
Take up the White Man's burden
In patience to abide
To veil the threat of terror
And check the show of pride;
By open speech and simple
An hundred times made plain
To seek another's profit
And work another's gain
Take up the White Man's burden
And reap his old reward:
The blame of those ye better
The hate of those ye guard
The cry of hosts ye humour
(Ah slowly) to the light:
"Why brought ye us from bondage,
"Our loved Egyptian night?"
Take up the White Man's burden
Have done with childish days
The lightly proffered laurel,
The easy, ungrudged praise.
Comes now, to search your manhood
Through all the thankless years,
Cold-edged with dear-bought wisdom,
The judgment of your peers.

Rudyard Kipling

GENERAL LUNA IS MURDERED BY AGUINALDO

Put Out of the Dictator's Way Because He Is Too Ambitious.

Special Dispatch to The Call.

MANILA, June 13.—General Antonio Luna, one of the bitterest foes of the Americans in the Philippines, has been assassinated by order of Aguinaldo.

Luna has recently found himself in opposition to the chief's views, and has not only disobeyed orders, but at one time stopped Aguinaldo's Peace Commissioners while on the way to treat with the Americans.

Aguinaldo ordered his death, and these orders were carried out by the Dictator's fanatical followers.

The report of the assassination caused great excitement among the Filipinos in Manila, which was added to later when the report was confirmed. The assassination of Luna occurred on June 8, at Kabanatuan,

GENERAL LUNA.

LONDON, June 13.—The Filipino Junta here confirms the story of the assassination of General Antonio Luna, and says it was the result of a long contest on the part of Luna against Aguinaldo. It is also said at the Junta that Agoncillo has returned to Paris from Rome, where he had an audience at the Vatican, and was told that a Filipino bishop might be appointed if the Fil-

A clipping from the San Francisco newspaper The Call kin June 1899

The Good General

General Antonio Luna was the best of the generals defending the new Philippine republic against the US in 1899, after the collapse of the Spanish administration. He was assassinated by other members of the Philippine leadership.

Cock-Fighting

An excerpt from The Former Philippines thru Foreign Eyes, *by Tomas de Comyn and others, published in 1917.*

The chief amusement of the Filipinos is cock-fighting, which is carried on with a passionate eagerness that must strike every stranger. Nearly every man keeps a fighting cock. Many are never seen out of doors without their favorite in their arms; they pay as much as $50 and upwards for these pets, and heap the tenderest caresses on them. The passion for cock-fighting can well be termed a national vice; but the practice may have been introduced by the Spaniards, or the Mexicans who accompanied them, as, in a like manner, the habit of smoking opium among the Chinese, which has become a national curse, was first introduced by the English. Probably Malay Custom.It is, however, more probable that the Malays brought the custom into the country. In the eastern portion of the Philippines, cock-fighting was unknown in the days of Pigafetta. The first cock-fight he met with was at Palawan. "They keep large cocks, which from a species of superstition, they never eat, but keep for fighting purposes. Heavy bets are made on the upshot of the contest, which are paid to the owner of the winning bird." The sight is one extremely repulsive to Europeans.

"Yes, Manila had its slums; one saw them on the drive from the airport: vast districts of men in dirty white undershirts lounging idly in front of auto-repair shops — like a poorer version of the 1950s America depicted in such films as Grease."

Author: Mohsin Hamid

Manila Cockroaches

American travel writer Burton Holmes commenting in 1905 on these formidable insects.

The bed is fortified with an elaborate mosquito-netting, dense enough to keep out the tiniest gnats, and at the same time strong enough to resist the onslaught of the flying cockroaches. The Manila insects of that name deserve a bigger name; they seem not insects, but athletic creatures, partaking of the nature of three classes — the crustacean, the rodent, and the raptores — an unhappy combination of lobster, rat, and vulture. By day they crawl on walls and tables, startling the stranger with their formidable aspect. At night after candles are extinguished, they begin aerial festivities. As they charge through the darkness from wall to wall, with a whizz and whirr, we seem to see the ride of the valkyries and hear their long Wagnerian shriek.

A map of Manila from 1898

Ruins and Romance

From Interesting Manila by George Miller. Publisher E.C. McCullough 1906

The globe trotter who spends two days doing Manila has no idea that he treads on the bones of a vanished empire. No field richer in romance is to be found than that which lies all about him and beneath his feet.

The Dwarf Angle

Don Santiago de los Santos was a Filipino dwarf who became part of a traveling show in England between the late 1820s and the early 1830s, and became a renowned individual in that place and time. The 1836 edition of the Mirror of Literature, Amusement and Instruction (Volume 28) said he was "....a native of the Spanish settlement of Manila; in one of the forests of which, it seems, he was exposed to death in his infancy, on account of his diminutive size. He, was, however, miraculously saved by the Viceroy, who, happening to be hunting in that quarter, humanely ordered him to be taken care of and nursed with the same tenderness as his own children, with whom the little creature was brought up and educated, until he attained the age of manhood."

An image from the 1830s of the famous Don Santiago

The Viceroy died when he was 20 years old, and the rest of the family turned their backs on him. He then "found his way to Madras, and was brought to England by the captain of a trading vessel." He was described as "stoutly built" and fond of "glittering attire, jewellery, and silver plate." Don Santiago was also multilingual: He could speak his native tongue as well as Indian patois, Portuguese, and English.

Santa Ana Cabaret

The cabaret concept, it is said, was brought to Manila during World War I by a German businessman married to an English lady.

The original idea was to cater to American guests, giving them a place to drink, dine and dance. But by the late 1920's, the concept of cabarets in Manila had shifted to be known as "dancing pavilions," far different in nature from the idea of catering to the American elite of Manila society.

In the 1920s, the Santa Ana Cabaret billed itself as the largest establishment of its kind of the world. It was owned by an American named John Canson, a Spanish-American War veteran, and the cabaret favored American guests while isolating Filipinos in the taxi-girl area away from the dinner-dance section. The Santa Ana Cabaret was destroyed in a typhoon in late 1970.

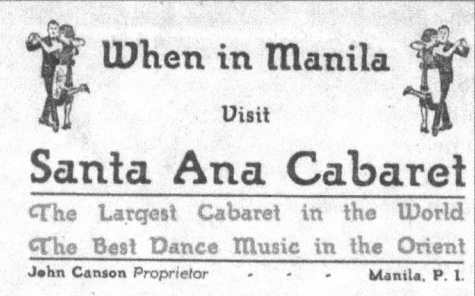

Banana Catsup

The revolutionary idea of making a sauce out of bananas, called banana catsup, belongs to Magdalo V. Francisco in 1938. It was a cheap alternative to tomato catsup (ketchup) because bananas are plentiful in the Philippines, and the taste is considered pleasant by Filipinos.

Banana Catsup

The End of the World

An article published in the Atlanta Constitution *in February 1902 on the health of Americans in the tropical Philippines. Amazingly, they were not dying like flies. Written by Joseph Ohl.*

Manila, Philippine Islands - One of the things which strikes a newcomer most forcibly upon his arrival at Manila is the apparent good health of the men he meets whom he has known before. Of the two of three hundred fellows I had known before I got here I have yet to find one who seemed any the worse for wear on account of the climate. Somehow there has grown up the conviction that white men cannot live in the tropics. There could be no greater mistake. True, people who have been reared in the temperate zone, and who have been used to winters must have an occasional taste of winter in order to preserve their intellectual vigor, but though a lot of army officers say they do not look any worse for their experience in the tropics. There is a general belief that this climate is injurious in that it takes away from a man his powers of recuperation and if he once starts down hill he is unable to stop himself. There may be something in this but it certainly is not true that white men have great difficulty in living their lives beneath the rays of the tropical sun. The idea that they do is one of the preconceived notions that a visit to this end of the world will drive out of your head.

A view of Rosario Street in the Binondo district of Manila, with the Binondo Church visible in the background. Taken around 1900.

The Evening Hour

*A charming Manila travelogue article entitled "Charming Sights at the Evening Hour",
published in* The Wilkes-Barre Record *in Pennsylvania in August, 1905.*

Manila, Aug. 9. – When the clock strikes 5 on any Wilkes-Barre morning winter or
summer, it is 6 o'clock in the evening at Manila of the Philippines and just thirteen
hours ahead. Manila has not only had it sunrise that has been passed on to the
Wilkes-Barre folks, but it has occupied itself with the business of the morning,
had luncheon, its afternoon siesta and its business, and finally the 6 o'clock hour
is enjoying the twilight and the life on the Luneta. This latter, is the most unique
park drive and walk in the world. The area of its lawn and boulevards covers
about ten acres and lies immediately at the edge of Manila Bay.

It is the twilight hour and its Luneta charm that brings the cream of Manila's
life to the Luneta at the hour of 2, before Wilkes-Barre residents are even thinking
of arising for their day's work. Westward over Manila Bay the sun is setting.
From across the bay softly blow the cool tropical evening breezes. The military
band at 6p.m. seated in their band stand in the centre of the Luneta promptly has
started their regular one-hour twilight concert. Thousands of Manila residents
are seated on the lawn or are strolling over the grass about the band stand and
thousands more in carriages are driving slowly up and down the boulevards
or standing along the curb listening to the music, enjoying the breeze and the
sunset over the bay. At no other city in the world is there such a scene of varied
peoples assembled under such picturesque and romantic surroundings and all
in common enjoying the beautiful tropical charm that pervades the Luneta at
the twilight hour.

Manila's elite is composed of many nationalities and when the Spaniards,
Americans, Filipinos, Germans, English, French, East Indian, Japanese, Chinese,
and most highly conspicuous over all, the American military in uniform and
white duck, all assemble and mingle together, it is almost as inspiring a sight as
was to Americans the news of Dewey's deed in Cavite Bay May 1, 1898.

Every night is the Luneta the rendezvous for this vast and widely varied
concourse of national representatives. And every night at the twilight hour they
look out over Manila Bay, with its 120 miles of circumference, on one of the finest
harbors in the world, so large as to be able to accommodate the combined fleets
of the entire European powers. The bay lies to the north and west of Manila.
It is chiefly to the westward that all eyes turned during many intervals of the
evening hour, for to the westward across the bay towering Marivales ridge of
mountains compels the setting sun to throw its golden reflections on the cloud
banks above, and it gives to the Luneta sojourners a nightly picture of gorgeous
sunsets never to be forgotten once they are seen.

In Foreign Lands

Mr Junkin wrote a travel article for the Adams County Free Press *in Iowa in June 1910, which interestingly begins be characterizing the Philippines as being part of "America".*

Manila, Philippine Island, March 22nd, 1910.

In America again! Oh, but it was good to see the people as we drew in to the dock at Manila. The smiling faces that were lifted to the decks on which we stood looked like home and our hearts grew warm as we looked at them and realized that we were being given a genuine American welcome by a crowd of our fellow countrymen. Oh! It was good, I tell you to get a breath from home again. I have always said that the best thing about going away is getting back home and this is applicable in the larger sense in which home means country as well as in a more restricted meaning; and these islands of the Pacific, far distant as they were, were America, and the people were glad to see us, as we were to see them.

A view over the San Fernando Bridge from Ermita of the Binondo Church, largely destroyed in fighting when the American re-took Manila in early 1944. Photo taken early 1900s.

The Far Eastern Championship Games

This annual competition foreshadowed all sorts of disputes and issues, and also cooperations. The first Far Eastern Championship Games took place in Manila in 1913, and its 10th and final iteration was held in 1934, when four entities took part – the Philippines, China, Japan and for the first time, the Dutch East Indies, one day to become Indonesia. India participated in 1925 but not thereafter. Of the 10 annual events, the Philippines captured the crown nine times, losing only once to China in 1921. In the 1934 event, held from May 16 to 20, a total of eight sports were contested. Women's events were included in the official medal count for the first time. The deterioration of relations between China and Japan disrupted the event from then on. Before the 1934 event, Japan repeatedly proposed that that Manchukuo compete as an independent team, which of course angered the Chinese, in that Manchukuo was a

Luis Salvador, a member of the basketball team that represented the Philippines in the 1923 Far eastern Games in Osaka. Note the symbol on his jersey - the Manila coat of arms from the Spanish era.

puppet state controlled by Japan following its invasion in 1931. A similar drama was to play out decades later with regard to Taiwan's involvement in sports events. The 11th Far Eastern Championship Games was scheduled to be held in 1938 in Osaka, but was cancelled after the 1937 outbreak of the Sino-Japanese War.

The Asian Games was held for the first time in 1951 and featured only two of the former Far Eastern group – Japan and the Philippines. China returned to the event in 1974.

A Promising Stay

The article entitled "Manila a promising field of labor" was written by YMCA grandee Robert Weidensall, who visited in 1906 to check on the Association's work in the new American colony. It was published in the Omaha Daily Bee on June 17, 1906.

DAMASCUS. Syria, May 19.- (Special Correspondense of The Bee.)- After leaving China I made a short but very interesting trip to Manila, Philippine Islands. I desired very much to stay longer, but did not have the time. I started from Hong Kong on December 27, 1906, on a small steam vessel, the Taning, and was about two and a half days in passage. Our vessel rolled and pitched in consequence of strong and constant northeast monsoon winds. All on board were more or less affected, including the ship's crew. It was the first voyage I had on any sea since I left San Francisco that compelled me to omit a single meal. It took much of the sentiment out of the song "Rocked in the Cradle of the Deep." We reached Manila harbor Saturday, December 30. Our ship was no sooner anchored than a multitude of small boats flocked about it with parties on board anxious to enter our ship as soon as the doctor and customs officer were through with it. A Fine white steam launch bearing the American flag, with an unusual set of men on it, was conspicuously present with the other smaller boats. All on our vessel watched it closely and wondered who the passengers were and what they wanted. The captain of our steamer could not tell who they were, but turned to me and said, "I don't know what they want unless it is yourself." As soon as they could they boarded our vessel and made their way up to the deck where I was standing and wanted to know if I was Secretary Weldensall. They proved to be Manila and army Young Men's Christian association folks, general secretaries and members of the board of directors of the Manila and army associations, including Dr. D. P. Barrows, president of the association, and Chaplain H. Swift. I need not say that I was accorded royal welcome. They soon had me and my things aboard the launch and steamed for the shore, where was a comfortable army conveyance which Chaplain Swift got from Major General Corbin and in which he took me to the Army and Navy club, where I lodged as the guest of the chaplain during my stay in Manila.

BAGOBOS WITH COMPLETE WAR EQUIPMENT

Image from a report prepared by the US administration in the early 1900s

Manila Folders

If you have ever wondered if the "Manila" in "manila envelope" and "manila folder" is associated with the Philippine capital, the answer is yes. Manila folders were originally made from the yellow-brown fiber from a species of plantain found only in the Philippines. This fiber was also made into "Manila rope" and reworked into "Manila hats". Today's manila folders and envelopes are made of ordinary paper, with a color designed to evoke the original.

Imelda Marco's collection of shoes, as found in the Presidential Palace in 1986

Doctrina Christiana

Believed to be one of the first books printed in the Philippines is the *Doctrina Christiana*. Written in 1593 by Fray Juan de Plasencia, the title literally means "Christian Doctrine," and the primary goal of the book was to propagate Christian teaching across the Philippines.

cover of Doctrina Christiana

A representation of a crocodile in the Pasig River from the book Adventures in the Philippine Islands, *by Paul P. de La Gironière, published in 1854*

The River That is Not a River

The Pasig River is central Manila's main watercourse, but it is actually not a river at all, but a tidal channel, and the flow of the water and the water levels are controlled by the ocean. It links the lake Laguna de Bay to Manila Bay. In recent decades, the Pasig has become hopelessly polluted.

The waterway is 25 kilometers in length, and was once infested with crocodiles. The book Relacion de las Islas Filipinas, by the Jesuit priest Pedro Chirino tells a story from the 17th-century of how a local tribal chief met and fought with a 36-foot crocodile by the Pasig River. The reptile was killed and when its stomach was ripped open, it was found filled with half digested human remains.

A postcard view of the Pais River, from around 1900

Water Buffalo Milk to Your Doorstep

Manila residents like drinking milk, and the milk they drank came from water buffalo, also known as carabao. The milk could be bought in local markets but most households preferred to have the milk delivered by "milk maids" who carried the milk in a pot on their heads.

The following is a passage from the book *The Governor-General's Kitchen: Philippine Culinary Vignettes and Period Recipes 1521-1935*, written by Felice Prudente Santa Maria, and relaying a description contained in the Spanish-language magazine La Ilustración Filipina, a Spanish language newspaper published in the 1890s.

A milkmaid "accepts monthly payments, and only in very special cases will ask for advanced payments." She usually carries an earthen jar on her head because "she is not used to carrying an umbrella, nor would she use it without running the risk of ruining her merchandise." The said jar was half-covered so as to prevent the milk from getting sour. A chupa was also placed at the jar's mouth which the milkmaid used for measuring. A Filipina milkmaid at that time was known for her professionalism, punctuality, and speed. It is said that milkmaids' "movements have a certain regularity resembling the handling of arms by the militia. She enters the house and hurriedly goes to the place for delivering milk. She stops like a soldier, lowers the earthen jar and the chupa (or half-chupa), which is always made of bamboo. She measures out the daily ration, returns the jar and chupa to their place, and goes off to the street in a flash, to repeat the described scene in the houses of all her other customers."

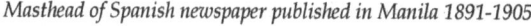

Masthead of Spanish newspaper published in Manila 1891-1905

The Manila Hotel

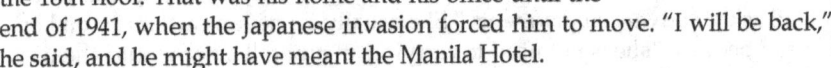

The Manila Hotel, built on reclaimed land next to Rizal Park, has played a central role in the city's history for more than a century. It was built on the orders of William Taft, then the Governor-General and later president of the United States, and was designed by New York architect William Parsons. It opened on U.S. Independence day, July 4, 1912 and was instantly the best hotel in the country.

In 1935, General Douglas MacArthur was appointed Military Adviser to the Philippine government, and he chose as his residence the penthouse suite of the hotel, on the 18th floor. That was his home and his office until the end of 1941, when the Japanese invasion forced him to move. "I will be back," he said, and he might have meant the Manila Hotel.

During the Japanese occupation, it provided accommodation for senior Japanese military officers, and when the US attack on Manila began in early 1945, the Japanese burned the hotel. The shell survived and was reconstructed.

During the Marcos era, the hotel was nationalized and it was a primary place of entertainment for the president's wife, Imelda. When the People's Power revolution toppled Marcos in 1986, some Philippine military officers occupied the hotel in support of his regime, but surrendered after two days. Today the 570-room hotel is majority owned by businessman Emilio Yap.

Manila Hotel in the 1920s

The Manila Hotel showing damage from the fighting in early 1945

Manila Hotel

Money

The first commercial bank in the Philippines was the Spanish establishment, El Bianco Espanol Filipino de Isabel II, opened in 1852. This bank also issued the first local banknotes in the territory.

The descendent and successor of that bank today is the Bank of the Philippine Islands (BPI).

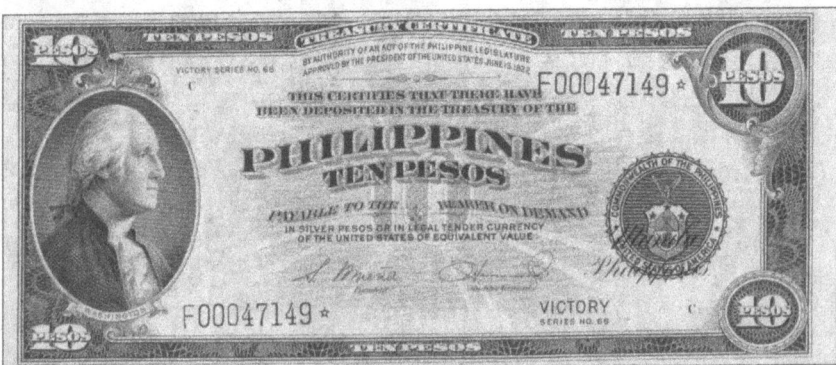

A postcard featuring Escolta Street, the main commercial thoroughfare of Manila, in the 1900s.

Salon de Pertierra

Filipinos are known for being movie fans, and the first films ever screened in the country, on January 1, 1897, were the following: Un Homme Au Chapeau (A Man with a Hat), Une Scène de Danse Japonnaise (Scene from a Japanese Dance), Les Boxers (The Boxers), and La Place de L' Opéra (Opera Plaza). They were shown using a 60 mm Gaumont Chrono-photograph projector at the Salon de Pertierra, a photographic studio.

PERTIERRA PHOTOGRAPH PARLORS

CARRIEDO, No. 46.

OLDEST IN MANILA.

All work guaranteed.
Flash Lights of Balls, Weddings, etc., etc.

Proprietors: *Sternberg Brothers*, Carriedo, No. 46.

High-Class Tagalog Girls

This image is from 1899. The text reads: "Women of this class understand the art of entertaining perfectly, and converse as fluently as the educated women of civilized countries. The mantels shown in the photograph are made of the elegant pina cloth, richly embroidered by hand, this work being done by the ladies themselves."

Pina Cloth

From Manila, The Burton Holmes Travelogues *by Burton Holmes. McClure 1908*

"There is little in the way of souvenirs and curios for which to spend one's money. The only native products that are tempting to travelers are the Filipino fabrics, the 'pina' cloth, made from the fiber of the pineapple leaf and a lovely fabric called 'jusi', part pine leaf and part hemp. Good pina is now hard to get, while all the prettiest designs in jusi have been picked up by early buyers."

- American travel writer Burton Holmes in 1905

> "I want the people of the Philippines to be happy, even if they have nothing."
> - Boxer Manny Pacquiao, who is currently serving as a Senator in the Philippines parliament

Finest Restaurant In Orient Owned By American Negro

By J. L. WALLER

Thomas Pritchard Opens New Grill in Manila; Is Show Place of Big City

Do You Know

Race Relations Sunday February Twelfth
ATLANTA, Ga., Dec. 29. — The

An article published in the *Philadelphia Inquirer* on December 31, 1927, telling the story of Tom's Oriental Grill, established in Manila by businessman Thomas Pritchard. The restaurant is described as "the finest and most luxurious culinary establishment and recreation center ever seen in the Philippines." The bar, it said, was imported from China and attracted much attention, "not only for its unique beauty but also for the liquors it yielded to those who visited it."

The Manila Carnival

The Manila Carnival was an annual event first held in 1908 by the American administration to provide entertainment and promote the commerical progress of the Philippines. The event lasted for two weeks, and was held on the old Wallace Field, close to today's Luneta Park. The crowning of the carnival queen was the climax of the event.

Queens of the Carnival

From the Manila Times, *March 3, 1908:*

"The first carnival ever to be held in the Philippines, which was supposed to end at midnight, finally came to a close early this morning in view of the enthusiasm of the thousands of people who thronged the fair grounds and stayed past the appointed hour. It was long after 2 a.m. that the crowds began to thin out. As the merrymakers filed slowly home, the lights of the carnival city dimmed for the last time thus ending six days and nights of revelry. In its issue for today, the Manila Times presents the observations of ranking government officials. Governor General James F. Smith is quoted as saying: "The carnival was an excellent success and far exceeded all expectations both from a financial and social point of view.""

Thomasites

In 1901, the United States government decided on an American education push in its new colony, the Philippines. More than 500 teachers were chosen and placed on a ship, the *USS Thomas*, which sailed from San Francisco in July, 1901, and arrived in Manila about one month later. The young people who chose to take the opportunity were motivated partly by money – the salary of US$125 per month was attractive in post-war America where unemployment rates were high – and altruism. The Filipinos dubbed this group the Thomasites. They taught English, mathematics, geography, housekeeping and household skills such as sewing and cooking. Many of the Thomasites suffered health problems due to their sudden exposure to the tropical climate, and more than 20 of them died in the first two years. The item below from a US newspaper in October of 1922 tells the story of how it played out for them.

REMAINING "THOMASITES" HOLD REUNION

Manila, P. I., Oct. 27.—Out of a total of 560 American teachers who came to the Philippine Islands on the United States transport Thomas, twenty-one years ago, only thirty-four remain in the Philippines, and only eight are still engaged in educational work. While the men outnumbered the women more than two to one, there being 400 men and only 160 women, the proportion has been radically changed until today virtually the entire American teaching corps in the islands is made up of women.

The thirty-four "Thomasites" as they are pleased to call themselves recently held a reunion, the twenty-first anniversary of their arrival in the islands.

A vintage wedding photo 1920s

Street Life

From Interesting Manila *by George Miller, 1906*

Few Americans can resist the interest found in the little Chino shops on Rosario and the *piña* stalls on San Fernando. It carries one back to the dreams of childhood when we saw hazy visions of little shops all our very own, where we would keep store when we got big and the folks would come and buy things of us. All the goods are in plain sight, and tools and bits of wire and hose and drygoods are all within reach. It's lots more fun than to go and sit on a stool while a man, pompous enough to be the lord mayor, approaches and with dignified condescension says, "What can I do for you?" I always feel like suggesting that he begin by deflating himself.

The Flexible President

The first president of the Philippines was Emilio Aguinaldo y Famy, who born in 1869, the son of the mayor of a town near Manila. He joined the revolutionaries secretly working to overthrow Spanish rule and in 1896 played a significant role in the first armed revolt again the Spanish, but after becoming the leader of the movement he did a deal with the Spanish and agreed to leave the Philippines for exile in Hong Kong in return for 400,000 pesos. He used the money to buy guns to continue the struggle. When the U.S. declared war on Spain in 1898, Aguinaldo hoped this would help the Philippines achieve independence, and he returned to Manila and declared Philippine independence on June 12. The United States made it clear it intended to rule the country, and although on January 1,

Emilio

1899 Aguinaldo was proclaimed president of the Philippine Republic, the US did not recognize his authority. On February 4, 1899 he declared war on the U.S. forces in the Philippines, and Agjuinaldo led an insurgency until he was captured on March 23, 1901. He then swore allegiance to the United States and left public life. He died in Manila in 1964.

Your Highness, Manila

From Interesting Manila *by George Miller. Publisher E.C. McCullough 1906*

Manila needs a guide book. Under her oriental exterior is hidden a wealth of historical material of highest human interest. In the very things that make many places famous among sightseers, she is easily the queen of the cities of the East, and for one who knows how to find the buried treasures, a year of residence in Manila may be one of the most profitable of a lifetime.

Eggs Are Off, Dear

Burton Holmes was one of the most prolific travel writers of all time, an American who gave lectures and wrote books about the many places he visited. He travelled through Hawaii and the Philippines in 1905. This is his description of breakfast at the Hotel de Oriente in Manila, in which he manages to insult the Filipinos, the Chinese and the English, all while talking about omelettes.

The best hotel in town is the Hotel de Oriente, but it is not admiration for that hostelry that impels me to write words which may be construed as words of praise. In hotel matters the superlative means nothing in Manila; the situation is completely hopeless. True, the structure is imposing, spacious, airy, and suggestive of coolness, comfort, and good cheer ; but these are vain suggestions. The table at this and every other place of public entertainment in Manila is impossible. True, the breakfast menu is rich in printed promises ; each dish is numbered to facilitate the task of giving orders to the Chinese waiters ; there are eight numbers. Let me run the gastronomic octave : —

1. PORRIDGE Watery gruel. We pass.
2. BEEFSTEAK Oriental beefsteak. We pass again ; but the subsequent items, despite a suggestion of monotony, seem to offer grounds for hope.
3. BOILED EGGS
4. SCRAMBLED EGGS
5. POACHED EGGS
6. OMELETTES
7. HAM AND EGGS
8. EGGS AND BACON

What more do you require? Very good; let us order No. 6.

"Boy, catchee me one piecee number six," is the command. The yellow garcon smiles a sad, cruel smile, and answers, "No have got eggs!" We are unfortunate in arriving just after the hotel has been taken over from the Spaniards by an English company. Prices have gone up, and the service has gone all to pieces. Chinese boys replace the Filipino waiters. The Spanish cuisine, good of its garlicky kind, has given place to a sort of emergency galley in charge of ignorant Celestials, and the only attempts at re-organization are confined to swearings, long and loud, on the part of the distracted manager. But as he swore in a new, unfamiliar language, his words were lost upon the servants, while the guests received the full force of his utterances. I paid ten dollars (Mexican) per day for the privilege of eating my own canned goods in the dining-room, and occupying a huge apartment overlooking the square.

A City of Many Words

Manila is a city of many languages, comprising the dozens of local languages spoken around the Philippines, all mutually unintelligible. But Tagalog is the predominant dialect of the Manila area, and hence now of the whole country. English is spoken by by 66.1%, and Spanish by 8.4%, the same survey indicated. Other languages include Iloco (4.9%), Samar-Leyte (3.3%), Pampango (3.0%), Bicol (2.8%), Chinese (2.6%), Cebuano (1.9%), Hiligaynon (1.9%), Pangasinan (1.7%).

Currency note showing the rice terraces of Luzon

An Englishman, A Spaniard and an American...

A quip from Charles B. Howard shortly after the Americans defeated the Spanish and took over the Philippines, published in "Frank Leslie's Popular Monthly," July-October 1898.

The saying goes in the Far East that if an Englishman, a Spaniard and an American were to be left upon a desert island, the first would organize a club, the second build a church, and the third start a newspaper."

Flying to the Philippines

The Philippines suddenly got a lot closer to the rest of the world on November 29, 1935. On that day, the first of the Pan American Airways "China Clipper" flying boats landed in Manila Bay after a flight from San Francisco lasting just under 60 hours. The plane was a Martin M-130 four-engine flying boat, built by the Glenn L. Martin Company in Baltimore, Maryland, and the aircraft was iconic of the progress being made in the 1930s in terms of international travel. One of the key reasons flying boats were practical in the mid-1930s was that there were very few air strips in existence, but the ocean was everywhere. Everything, including aviation, changed as a result of World War Two. The China Clipper reached Manila via Honolulu, Midway Island, Wake Island, and Guam. When it landed, within sight of the Manila Hotel, it powered up to a special pontoon that had been constructed to receive it. The last commercial flight by one of the planes took place in January 1945.

The first Pan-Am China Clipper flight after it landed in Manila Bay in November 1935

Hysterical Welcome

From the diary of the US Governor-General F.B. Harrison:

"Arrival at 3:30 p.m. of the China Clipper–the first commercial airplane on the United States-China service. Like a great silver bird. Tremendous excitement –women rather hysterical. Perfect landing of the big plane in the harbor. Simultaneous arrival of the French Admiral on his ship. Everyone mistook the salutes for the Admiral as being a tribute to the plane"

Pan Am China clipper landing in Manila Bay

What's in a Name

The book Manila and the Philippine Islands, *published by The Philippines Company of New York in 1899, explains how the Philippines got its name.*

"In 1564 Don Miguel Lopez de Legazpi sailed with an expedition from Brazil and founded a Spanish settlement where the town of Cebu now is. It was then that the islands were named the Philippines in honor of Philip II, then King of Spain."

Whips and Buckles

An item from the book Seaports of the Far East, *published in 1907, praising a famous shop in old Manila specializing in leather goods, saddles and whips.*

Riu Hermanos ad

The variety and character of the innumerable articles pertaining to modern commerce is a subject on which many volumes could be written. Among these there is none that is more useful than leather. The versatility of its use is shown by the stock in Messrs. Riu Hermanos' establishment at 153-155 Escolta. This firm are specialists in leather goods of all kinds. Messrs. Riu Hermanos' assortment of saddles manifests the perfection to which these articles have been brought, and include all kinds for both ladies and gentlemen - soft and elastic seats that greatly enhance the pleasure of equestrian exercise.

No less worthy is their display of harness, which comprises every item and device that makes for the comfort of the horse, the improvement of its appearance, and the reduction of its labour between the shafts. Whips, spurs, and stable requisites of every description are also largely in evidence, together with sporting goods. Repairs and orders for leather manipulation of all kinds are skilfully and promptly executed by experts, under the personal supervision of the proprietors, Messrs. J. and J. Riu. They have been established in Manila about fourteen years and their establishment adds considerably to the attractiveness and utility of the Escolta.

Riu Hermanos store front

Deutcheland in Manila

German residents of Manila established the Deutscher Klub or German Club on January 16, 1906, and it did well until 1917 when the United States entered the war against Germany, closed the club and interned all German residents. In the 1920s, the club was revived, and saw its heyday in the 1930s.

The German Club in 1931

A street scene in old Manila, around 1900

Spanish Water-boarding

George A. Miller, in his book Interesting Manila *published in 1906, talks about the Fort Santiago as it was found by the Americans who took Manila from the Spanish in 1898, and for a time made Fort Santiago their military headquarters.*

"There are all sorts of stories floating about the old fort. So far as the walls are concerned, there is some foundation for the stories. There are storerooms and magazines, and the outer curtains are connected with the main wall in some cases by underground passages, or were, before these tunnels were destroyed. The filling of the old moat closed them, probably forever. When the wall at the end of Calle Aduana was removed, the inner chamber was found filled with human skeletons. There were however, underground passages and deep-built cells in the fort itself. When the Americans took charge of the place (in 1899) there was no opening in the wall where the large stairway is now located on the river face, but from the large room now used as a magazine there was a circular well just under the new stairway. This well was entered by means of a series of winding stone steps, and led down to a passage considerably below the level of the water in the river. This lower passage led back from the river and was lined on each side by cells which could be closed from the front and which were so low that it was impossible to stand in them. There was also a movable gate by which the water could be admitted from the river, and all the evidence pointed to the use of these cells for purposes of "unintentional" executions of persons whom it would be expedient to have out of the way without open trial or public capital punishment. The natives have a terror of this old place and have no desire to see anything below the surface of the walls."

Fort Santiago showing the moat that surrounded it for centuries. See the American flag flying from the walls, This photo was probably taken in 1899

The main gate to Fort Santiago, as it was in 1930

William Taft, 27th President of the United States, on a carabao in Manila in 1902

Governor Taft

William Howard Taft served as President of the United States from 1909 to 1913, but prior to that he spent around two years in the Philippines, from 1900 to 1903, mostly in the role of civilian governor.

Taft was aware that many Filipinos had been disappointed when the US did not support independence after the Spanish left in 1898, and instead ran it as their own colony, and he proposed that a path to self-government be created. He noted that many Americans viewed Filipinos as their racial inferiors, and said he intended "to banish this idea from their minds."

Taft also proposed fundamental land reform giving Filipino farmers rights to their land, held then, and largely still today, by major land-owners.

The General

Douglas Macarthur's relationship with the Philippine extended back to his father, also a military man, who was posted to the newly-occupied territory in 1898 and commanded the fight against the Philippine independence forces led by Emilio Aguinaldo's revolutionaries, who included Macarthur's future friend, Manuel Quezon. MacArthur the father was the commander of the Army of the Philippines, but during those years, Douglas was the United States, preparing to enter the West Point military academy.

Douglas first saw action in France in World War I and made a name for himself even then as someone willing to challenge his superiors, a trait that, along with arrogance would one day cause his downfall. As the New York Times obituary on April 6, 1964, a classic piece of journalism, put it: "The man who demanded and got complete obedience to his orders on the part of subordinates did not always apply the military golden rule to himself."

Time Magazine featured General Douglas Macarthur on the front cover a number of times during the 1940s and early 1950s. This cover, from August 1942, soon after his retreat from Manila, included this quote: "On to Tokyo for the peace of the world".

Macarthur's response, then and always, was that he was "animated by the sole desire to help restore. preserve and advance those great American principles and ideals of which we have been beneficiaries ourselves and are not trustees for future generations."

After an illustrious career in the peacetime military between the wars, In October, 1935, MacArthur was sent to the Philippines as military adviser to the newly semi-independent country, and he worked to build a force there that could defend the islands against the growing threat of Japan. In August, 1937, he was ordered to return to the United States to take up another military post back home, and his response was to resign, saying his John in the Philippines was not yet finished. His resignation was accepted, and the Philippines president, Manuel Quezon, immediately appointed him Field Marshal of the Philippines. On the basis of that rank, MacArthur designed his unique military cap that, along with sunglasses and his corncob pipe, became his trademark.

> General Douglas Macarthur, February 22, 1942:
> "I shall return."
> General Douglas Macarthur, October 30, 1944:
> "I have returned. By the grace of Almighty God, our forces stand again on Philippine soil."

The New York Times said: "His considerable investments, both in the Philippines and in this country, were the basis of frequent conjecture, but their extent and nature were never disclosed. His mode of living after achieving top rank was such that he seldom opened a door, drove an automobile or had to perform the myriad personal tasks of ordinary persons." Which may explain why he declined to return to the United States in 1937.

With the possibility of war with Japan rising, the Philippine Army was merged with the United States Army, and MacArthur was restored to a point in the American military as a lieutenant general on July 27, 1941. He was promoted to full general 11 days after the Japanese attack on Pearl Harbor.

MacArthur concentrated his forces in the US military base on the Bataan Peninsula, north of Manila, and the Japanese, who attacked the Philippines immediately with well-trained units, aimed straight for Bataan. The battle lasted five months, with the US force surrendering on May 5, 1942. MacArthur, however had exited early,. Under orders, he and his wife, their four-year-old-son and a Chinese nanny, left his headquarters on the island of Corregidor on a PT boat that made it through the Japanese naval blockade.

"I shall return," he said.

He went to Australia as the commander of US forces in the Asia-Pacific theater, and his goal was the first liberate the Philippines, even though this was not necessarily the best strategy.

His plan was to use the Philippines as the springboard for an attack on Japan, and said the United States was "honor-bound" to liberate the Philippines. At a meeting in July 1944, he convinced President Roosevelt to do just that. The alternative plan, supported by the US Navy, was to attack and liberate Taiwan and parts of China first.

On Oct. 30, 1944, two and a half years after he left, MacArthur waded ashore at Leyte and said: "I have returned." Manila fell after a vicious four-month fight with huge civilian losses, on February 25, 1945.

macarthur7

A Wandering Race

This notice from the Japanese military authorities in Manila warning the Jews to behave, was included in Frank Ephraim's book, Escape to Manila.

WARNING
NON-COLLABORATING JEWS IN THE PHILIPPINES
TO BE DEALT WITH DRASTICALLY
January 25, 1943

In keeping with the spirit of Hakko Itiu (Universal Brotherhood), Japan does not discriminate against any particular race of people. Hitherto, she has adopted just and tolerant measures regarding the treatment of enemy nationals.

However, it was to the greatest regret of the Japanese Military Administration that among the Jews—a part of the third-party nationals (irrespective of their nationality)—there were some who committed refractory and arrogant acts, abusing the benevolent measures of the Imperial Forces, and were therefore subsequently punished.

The Jews, as we all know, are people without a motherland; they are a wandering race. They are parasites of the countries in which they live. Due to this circumstance they ought to be more faithful than the other nationals in respecting the traditions and laws of the countries in which they reside.

However, the facts have proven this to be the opposite. ... There are indications among Jewish residents of the Philippines of the following activities: hoarding of commodities for the purpose of raising commodity prices, exploiting Filipino women, participation in espionage activities, and otherwise behaving out of harmony with the policies of the Japanese Military Administration.

We hereby issue a solemn warning that if activities such as those enumerated above are discovered, the perpetrators will be dealt with most drastically by the Japanese Military Administration irrespective of whether the Jews have nationality or not and without regard to the country of which they are nationals.

We add here that regarding the profiteering conducted by a section of recalcitrant Chinese, the Japanese Military Administration has issued strict warning through the Chinese Association.

JAPANESE MILITARY ADMINISTRATION

A private home on Escolta Street, photographed in 1871

Open City

"Open City" was declared on December 26, 1941 by the U.S. Commander Douglas MacArthur in an effort to prevent Japanese attacks on the city. "This declaration is another way of saying that Manila is not under the Americans or anyone anymore so stop attacking it," he declared.

Manila declared an open city

119

Manila Shawls - Mantones de Manila

The Manila Shawl is an exquisite merging of European and Oriental elements which was long a sought-after luxury item in the West. The basic design, a large square shawl with a fringe, is Spanish, but the best Manila shawls are made out of Chinese silk and are embroidered with intricate Oriental designs, often dragons, birds and flowers in a Chinese style. They were first shipped eastwards across the Pacific to Acapulco on the return trips of the Manila Galleons, and from there were on-shipped to Europe.

The Battle of Manila, 1945

In late 1941, when the Japanese invaded the Philippines, then an American colony, General Douglas MacArthur, commander of the U.S. forces there, declared Manila an 'open city' to spare it from destruction. But when the Americans returned in early 1945, the Japanese decided to fight to the last man, and burned entire city blocks to stem the American advance. The battle lasted for a month, from February 3 to March 3 1945, and was the worst urban fighting in the Pacific war. The result was the death of over 100,000 residents and the complete devastation of the city. Manila is considered by some to be the second-most devastated city in World War II after Warsaw, Poland.

MacArthur in the rubble

The Legislative Building in 1945, after the fighting

Memorial

On February 18, 1995, the Shrine of Freedom was dedicated in memory of the war dead. The monument is located at the Plaza de Santa Isabel, on the corner of General Luna and Anda Streets in Intramuros, Manila. The inscription reads:

"This memorial is dedicated to all those innocent victims of war, many of whom went nameless and unknown to a common grave, or even never knew a grave at all, their bodies having been consumed by fire or crushed to dust beneath the rubble of ruins. Let this monument be the gravestone for each and every one of the over 100,000 men, women, children and infants killed in Manila during its battle of liberation, February 3 - March 3, 1945. We have not forgotten them, nor shall we ever forget. May they rest in peace as part now of the sacred ground of this city: the Manila of our affections."

I Wouldn't Go in There

From all the stories, there must be a lost of ghosts in the Philippines, but the place that gets top billing in terms of hauntedness is an abandoned hospital near Clark Air Force base, in Angeles City, near Manila.

The Clark airbase hospital

The Beauty of the Women of Manila

Fedor Jagor, who visited Manila in 1959, had this to say on the females of the city:

"In the comeliness of the women, who lend animation to its streets, Manila surpasses all other towns in the Indian Archipelago. It is really so: the contrast to the Javans and women of Singapore is very great, and among the "Mestizos," or half-castes of the Visayas, there are numbers who can hold there own with any Europeans, whilst among the pure Indians there are multitudes of really pretty faces set off by luxuriant black hair and dark eyes. At a fiesta one comes across a very fine spectacle in the numbers of pretty women in their bright coloured "sayas" (petticoats') of every hue, and pure white pina "camisas " of delicate workmanship, black lace "mantilla," and dainty slippers without heels, and beautifully embroidered."

Filipino women dressed in their best

122

From Tomas to Bãnos

On May 8, 1943, the Japanese military commandant of the Santo Tomas Internment Camp for enemy aliens in Manila, issued this statement, ordering the move of hundreds of internees to a new camp at Los Banos, which was one of the first locations in Luzon to be liberated in February 1945 by American troops.

I am authorized by the Director-General of the Japanese Military Administration in the Philippines to make a statement regarding the change of location of enemy civilian's internment camp. As all of you are well aware, released enemy nationals in the city of Manila are more than 2,000. Most of them, being unemployed, are in extreme difficulties in their living, and the number of applicants for internment is daily increasing. It is, however, to be pointed out that the present accommodations available in the Santo Tomas Internment Camp is not sufficient to have all of them interned there, and particularly so from sanitary point of view.

In consideration of these facts, the [Japanese] Military Authorities here have come to a decision, to change the location of the internment camp to a more spacious place where more permanent accommodations can be provided so that you will continue to live there until the time when you will repatriate to your respective countries or peace will be restored.

The new site is in Los Baños, Laguna, an ideal health resort noted for its hot springs, where new buildings will be erected for your housing and where you will enjoy fresh air and find easy access to fresh meat and vegetables, part of which you may be able to cultivate yourselves.

In carrying out the above plan, the first group of about 800 men to be selected from the present internees, which will constitute the core for the new camp, will be dispatched to Los Baños by trains on the 14th of the month. For this first group, the premises of the Agriculture College including its large track field will be available.

It is to be emphasized that this change of location is entirely based upon the humanitarian consideration of your own welfare, and that fairness to the treatment to be accorded to internees shall always be maintained.

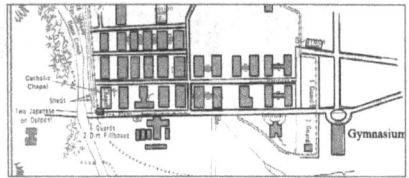

Baker Hall in the Los Bãnos camp   *Los Bãnos camp map*

The Santo Tomas Internment Camp

The University of Santo Tomas was established in Manila in 1611, but it was not until 1942 that it gained widespread attention, when it was requisitioned by the Japanese occupying forces as an internment camp for foreigners. From January 1942 until the camp was liberated by U.S. forces in February of 1945, more than 3,000 internees were kept in the camp in conditions that became steadily worse as the woman progressed.

The Marines vs Starvation

An entry from The Santo Tomas Internment Camp Diary of Albert E. Holland, 1944-1945

Nov. 17th. What I have expected has come to pass – our camp reserves of rice are exhausted. And starting tomorrow we will receive only 225 grams of cereal daily – nothing else – This is equal to about 950 calories – 1/3 of what we need – The children will have some milk and vegetables, so that they will have about 1100 calories, about 55% of what they need – Of course, the diet is mostly carbohydrates – there is little

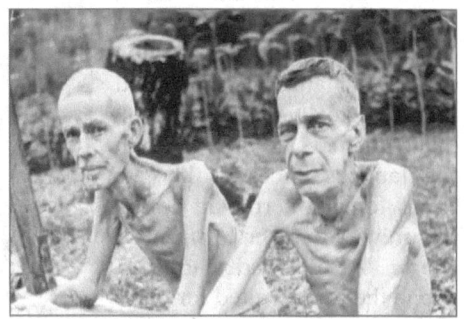

Two extremely emaciated American civilians at the Santo Tomas camp in February 1945.

protein in rice & corn – But we get no meat, no sugar, almost no vegetables, no fruit, no coffee, no tea – three scoops of mush for breakfast, 1 scoop of soft boiled rice (lugao) for lunch and 1 scoop of rice or corn for supper- I weigh 110 today – Down 18 pounds in 17 days - 81 pounds below my pre-war weight – "Good humor is the finest mark of courage" There is one thing we have that the Japanese have not: Hope – I would rather have 950 calories a day & hope than 3000 calories & despair. And many people, millions are starving throughout the world. In Poland, Germany, Denmark, Belgium, France China & here in the P.I. The Japanese are not eating well. So the struggle enters its crucial stage – The Marines against Starvation.

Liberation

An excerpt from the book Surviving a Japanese Internment Camp *by Rupert Wilkinson.*

3 February 1945. It was after nightfall when six U.S. Army Sherman tanks with an assortment of jeeps and trucks trundles into Calle España, the street running past the main gate of the old Dominican University of Santo Tomás. They waited there while more trucks came up. The force numbered 200 GIs, led by a lieutenant colonel, Haskett Hack Conner. They were the frontrunners of a "flying column" of tanks and motorized infantry – really a series of small detachments - cutting through the Japanese lines to liberate Santo Tomás Internment Camp, the university turned prison for nearly 4,000 Allied nationals. While the force waited for more

The Santo Tomás grounds following liberation

tanks to show up (some got lost), the camp seemed strangely quiet. There was no movement from the guardhouse just inside the gate. No lights from the Main building, a stone and concrete structure whose massive tower and tall crucifix dominated the camp. A sizzling sound like a firecracker broke the silence. A Japanese soldier had stepped out of the guardhouse and thrown a grenade. Two GIs shot him dead through the railings, but the grenade had found targets. Shrapnel gashed Colonel Conner's leg and mortally wounded Captain Manuel Colayco, one of two Filipino guerrillas who helped guide the Americans through the city. There was no time to wait for reinforcements. The lead tank, "Battlin' Basic," scraped through the gate's arch, showering bits of masonry onto the helmets of riflemen walking beside it. The camp broke into life as jubilant, cheering internees tumbled out of the Main Building to meet the tanks.

*Two boys watch as US field gunners fire from Santo Tomás grounds at
Japanese artillery positions in Manila,*

Domes and Cupolas

From Interesting Manila *by George Miller, published in 1906*

Manila is a city of churches. Her skyline, seen from the bay, is an outline of domes and cupolas, and above all surrounding buildings blaze the corrugated roofs of her Christian temples. China has her walls, India her pagodas, her carved shrines and gilded images, but the distinguishing feature of Manila is her churches. She alone of all the cities of the East, is rich in the sanctuaries and symbols of the faith of the civilized world.

Binondo cathedral in 1948

A Navigator

An excerpt from a story called "On The Consequence of Sound" by Timothy Dimacali, published in the book "The Sea is Ours, by Rosarium Publishing in 2015

To live in Intramuros was to live surrounded by music. I remember fondly one cold summer morning under a clear blue sky many years ago, when I was just a little child back in the old Walled City. My father, holding my hand, took me to our balcony to greet the new day. I was too small to look over the ledge, too scared to look down. So I just closed my eyes and listened — to the dawn hymns of the monks singing in their chapels high up in the rascacielos, the clacking of horses' hooves on the cobblestoned streets far below, the throaty cries of the Sangley street vendors echoing from the alleys, the rhythmic thumping of mortars on pestles as the day's rice was being prepared. All around us, Intramuros was alive with the sounds of ritual and habit: a strong, steady heartbeat that had remained unchanged for centuries. It was the sound of home, of life within the Walls. Suddenly, Papa shook my shoulder.

"Look there, Aria!"

My curiosity got the better of me. I opened my eyes to find him pointing into the distance, out across the bay. The Nuestra Señora del Cielo was a sight to behold as it came in to port. The royal galleon's masts, each thick around as the torsos of seven men, seemed to defy the very sky itself. Her massive wooden hull, made from the most ancient and darkest narra wood and inlaid with gold and mother of pearl, cast a long shadow over the houses and churches beneath it. The whole city, it seemed, fell into silent awe at the sight of the great ship flying in from the sea. A squadron of smaller, sliver-shaped escort ships flew in tight formation ahead of it, their linen sails billowing at full mast, white as clouds. Each escort glinted with its own complement of brass lantaka cannons extended in ceremonial salute. The Navigators of the entire retinue, sight unseen, played at a steady tempo as they guided their ships on course. I will always remember the music of their viols descending from the air, a cascade of notes that swelled and receded in wave after grand wave of sonorous rapture, announcing the arrival of the royal galleon. It was then that I knew I would become a Navigator.

A photo from March 1946, celebrating the first anniversary of the liberation of Manila from the Japanese by American forces. The GIs and the locals are ready for their ice creams.

The Post-War Era

Filipino Film Stars

The 1950s was the "Golden Age" for the Filipino film scene. The first movie was actually screened for an audience in Manila in 1897, and a British entrepreneur set up the first dedicated cinema in 1900. The first indigenous movie was made in 1919, entitled "Country Maiden". Both film production and cinema attendance surged in the 1930s, and the Philippines has ever since had one of the highest cinema attendance levels in the world. The Japanese occupation in late 1941 brought production to almost a complete halt, and cinemas were basically required to show only Japanese films. Then with the return of the Americans in early 1945, the way was clear for a movie boom.

The industry was organized much like Hollywood, with a studio system, approved stars and almost no independent production. The FAMAS (Filipino Academy of Movie Arts and Sciences) preseted its awards for the first time in 1952, Stars included Amalia Fuentes, dubbed the "Filipino Elizabeth Taylor". Fernando Poe Jr, known as the "King of Philippine movies", had his first hit in 1957 at the age of 18, and climaxed his career by running for president in 2004. Other stars from this era include Eddie Garcia, Tita Duran (a child star), Marlene Dauden, and Pancho Magalone, who was also husband to Tita Duran.

Jose Mari Gonzales

Marlene Dauden

Eddie Garcia

Fernando Poe, Jr.

Tita Duran

Dolphy

Rosa Rosal

Amalia Fuentes

Wack Wack

This was both the popular name for a small nine-hole golf course on Malecon Drive (now Bonifacio Drive), linking Intramuros with the port area of Manila, and also the cry given by a golfer before hitting the ball. It is said the name came from the cry of ravens who were scared by a stray ball - the phrase "uwak uwak" in Tagalog is associated ravens. In any event, on that course, the traditional "Fore!" was replaced by "Wack! Wack!"

wack wack

The Wack Wack clubhouse, which was destroyed by fire before World War II. A second and larger clubhouse was built,m which also burned to ground.

The Binondo Church in Manila, originally built in 1596. It was destroyed by a British naval bombardment in 1762 and was rebuilt in 1852, but was again badly damaged during the American attack on Japanese-held Manila in February 1944.

The Help

David Byrne is best known as the leader of the band Talking Heads, but is also a manic cyclist and has ridden a bicycle across much the world. In 2009, he published a book called Bicycle Diaries, which included the following comment.

The Philippines, for many Americans, is the land where maids and nurses come from, and that's about all they know about it. I have to admit I've seen quite a lot of men and women in medical attire. Filipinos are hopeful that Japan, for example, might employ some of their highly trained medical personnel, but the Japanese are notoriously uncomfortable dealing physically with foreigners, and the idea of being touched by one, God forbid! The Japanese instead prefer to develop robot to take care of their own mundane housekeeping and medical needs. Racism as a spur to technical innovation.

The Beatles Fiasco

In mid-1966, at the height of the first phase of their fame, the Beatles were in the midst of a world tour that took them to Japan, Hong Kong, Sydney and Manila. In Manila, they played two shows to crowds of the usual screaming teenagers numbering over 100,000 in total. The sound quality was, again as usual, appalling, and the screaming of the fans drowned out the efforts of the band to communicate much beyond a sense of cute, youthful musical energy. This tour, and particularly the Philippines leg of it, resulted in the decision by the Fab Four to stop touring altogether and restrict their musical activities to the studio. The story of what happened in their brief two-day visit to the Philippines does not reflect well on anyone except John, Paul, George and Ringo, who were caught up in some-time totally beyond their control.

The Beatles live in Manila

The group arrived in Manila on July 3, 1966 from Tokyo, the second stop on the Asian tour, the first of its kind by any Western pop group. The local promoter was Ramon Ramos of Cavalcade International Promotions, and it is important to remember that at the time, Ferdinand Marcos had been president of the Philippines for only one year, and that his wife Imelda was extremely interested in the concept of celebrity.

Ramos, the promoter, sent a telegram to the Beatles' manager Brian Epstein while the group was in Tokyo informing him that it had been arranged that the Beatles would make a courtesy call on Mrs Marcos at the Presidential Palace as soon as they arrived in Manila. Ramos says he received no reply to this message, and assuming acceptance, he finalized plans for the event. Things did not go well. Imelda prepared a lavish luncheon and invited hundreds of people including senators, congressmen, cabinet secretaries and other VIPs. But the Beatles, when they landed and heard of the arrangement, declined to attend. The following day, July 4, 1966, the Beatles performed twice at Rizal Memorial Stadium. It was a standard and short set, 10 songs, less than 30 minutes in total. Not a particularly musical event, which in retrospect is a huge shame given the musical leanings of the Philippines. But the following day, when they departed, chaos erupted.

Some say that the madness at

Manila Airport as the Beatles left was orchestrated by Imelda, but on the other hand Manila Airport has never, and to this day, been noted for calm efficiency. When the group reached the airport, no one helped them with their luggage, the escalator was turned off, and all VIP privileges were denied them. According to one witness, the Beatles, Brian Epstein and the rest of their party were "jostled, kicked and punched as they made their way to the departure gate." Epstein was forced to surrender $17,000 cash to the authorities before they were allowed to leave. Imelda, not unexpectedly, had a different explanation. In a statement published in the *Philippine Star*, she said that she had nothing to do with the airport troubles. She also said that when she heard that the group was being mishandled by disappointed Filipinos at the airport, "I immediately ran to the airport to have it stopped." The image of Imelda running to the airport is engaging. "I would never dream of hurting the world's No. 1 band," she added, possibly with sincerity. "Whatever motivated the people to treat them that way was not my doing. They could have done it out of sympathy and I think it was wrong. I abhor violence."

More Wealthy Than Lahore

A comment from Pakistani author Mohsin Hamid, author of books including The Reluctant Fundamentalist, *published in 2007.*

"I tried not to dwell on the comparison; it was one thing to accept that New York was more wealthy than Lahore, but quite another to swallow the fact that Manila was as well."

Mythical Creatures of the Philippines

Christianity plays a major role in the lives of most Filipinos, and Islam a key part of the lives of many in the south of the country. But the animist beliefs that predate both imported religions are still fundamental to the fantasy world of the Philippines. These beasts are not visible to everyone, and the explanation for that is that only the good and the pure can see them. The beasts include:

Bakunawa - a dragon that sometimes appears as a gigantic sea
Bungisngis - a happy one-eyed giant that lives in the forest.
Aswangs - shapeshifters, look like humans during the day and turn into animals or monsters during the night, often blackbirds or bats. They prey on people who are asleep, especially pregnant women. The only way to keep this creature away is to put broom stick upside down.
Diwata (from Sanskrit devada, "gods") - spirits that guard forests, mountains and plots of land. They can bring blessings or curses on those who do good or harm to Nature.
Duwende - goblins, elves or dwarfs (Spanish: duende "goblin). They are little creatures who can provide good or bad luck to people. Before the Spanish came, they were called mangalo. They live in houses or in trees, and can be good or bad, depending on how people treat them..
Ekek - winged creatures that search for victims at night, hungry for flesh and blood.
Garuda - a large bird-like creature with the upper body of a man and the face and wings of a great bird. They also live in Indonesia's fantasy world.
Kapre - a giant who smokes big cigars and lives in trees.
Naga - fresh-water mermaids, with human female heads and bodies but their tails are those of eels or snakes, not fish.
Mambabarang (summoner) - a witch who uses insects and spirits to enter the body of any person they hate.
Manaul - a mythical king who became a bird. He caused the seas and the skies to fight against each other, and the clash resulted to the creation of the Philippine islands.
Mangkukulam - witches and wizards who cast evil spells on humans.
Multo - ghosts, often a spirit of a deceased relative.
Nuno sa punso - goblins who live in small bumps in the ground. Superstitious Filipinos, when passing a mound, will ask the nuno's permission first.
Sarangay - a creature that looks like a bull with a big body and a jewel attached to its ears.

Sarimanok - a magical bird that brings good luck to anyone able to catch it.
Tamawo - mythical creatures, handsome and with white skin, fangs and claws of gold.
Tikbalang - a half-man and half-horse creature with a horse's head, the body of a human and the feet of the horse. It prowls around at night looking for human girls to rape.
Wakwak - a flying creature that inhabits rural areas and will attack people, and eat their hearts.

Bull-fighting

The Spanish brought the bloody sport of bullfighting to Manila during the late 19th century. Trumbull White, in his 1898 book, *Our New Possessions*, wrote:

"The sports of Manila are materially different from those to which we are accustomed, for their favorites have been bullfighting and cock-fighting. The bull ring in Manila, in the suburb of Paco, draws great crowds when the entertainment is offered, in spite of the fact that the performances are by no means spirited. Neither Spanish bullfighters nor Spanish bulls are brought to the island, so that native talent has to be obtained for both roles. The bulls are timid and lazy, the bull-fighters are little better so that the traveler does not see bullfighting of the same sort that he would in Spain, Cuba or Mexico."

Manila bullfight

Bullfighting in Manila, 1890s

Thrilla in Manila

The boxing match between Muhammad Ali and Joe Frazier in Manila in 1975 was one of the most celebrated fights in history. It took place on October 1 in Manila, but it was Sept 30 in the United States. It was oppressively hot, close to 100 degrees Fahrenheit. Ali seemed to tire after the first few rounds, but he recovered in the 12th round, and scored some brutal punches to Frazier's face and head in rounds 13 and 14. Frazier' trainer would not let Frazier get back up at the start of the 15th round, so Ali won, but the fight was clearly a huge strain for him. Asked afterwards, Ali said the flight was "the closest thing to dying that I know."

It will be a killa
And a chilla
And a thrilla
When I get the gorilla
In Manila
-Muhammad Ali's taunt to Joe Frazier

Thrilla in Manila, with Ferdinand and Imelda Marcos present

"This fight could make a legitimate claim to being the greatest fight of all time, maybe not in terms of social significance, but in terms of great action between two historic fighters."

- Author Thomas Hauser

Caseos and Modesty

A diary entry from My Mother's Journal; a young lady's diary of five years spent in Manila, Macao, and the Cape of Good Hope from 1829-1834, *by Harriet and Katharine Hillard, published in 1900, describing arrival in Manila Bay. Caseo was a word meaning small covered boat, a close relation of the sampans of the China coast.*

September 8. – A pleasant morning, though it looks as though it would rain before night. I was on deck early, and it was a pleasant prospect, I assure you. The Cavite (where ships usually anchor in the south-west during monsoons) on one side and Manila on the other. The caseos look quite lively, with the natives going about from one to another. These caseos are dug out of trees, and have a covering of bamboo, under which the family live. In one the wife was rowing. I should not have known her to be a woman at first, as she had on nothing but trousers. The men are merely covered about the middle.

The Tale of the Pearl of Allah

What was then the world's largest pearl was discovered in the Palawan Sea in 1934. It was variously known as the "Pearl of Lao Tzu," (a Chinese philosopher) or the "Pearl of Allah". It weighed fourteen pounds and the Filipino diver who found it died in the jaws of the clam that gave birth to the pearl. It was taken to the United States in 1939 by Wilburn Cobb. The pearl is mis-shapen and looks more like a brain than a traditional pearl.

From the article "The Pearl of Allah" by Wilburn Cobb, published in 1939.

When I first saw the pearl I could hardly believe my eyes. There on the table in front of us lay the largest pearl ever beheld by human eyes. The gigantic gem weighed fourteen pounds, one ounce. It was nine and a half inches long and five and a half inches in diameter, and glowed with a highly reflective, satiny sheen.

Two more attendants entered, carrying the half of the shell in which the pearl was found, and the old Panglima laid the pearl in its former bed. It seemed as though I were looking at a pearl that might have been taken from the pages of the Arabian Nights. I asked my host to name his price, but was kindly but firmly told that the pearl was not for sale. Smilingly, the Panglima said, "It would be a sacrilege for me to part with this pearl. A pearl with the image of Mohammed, the Prophet of Allah, is earned by devotion, by sacrifice, not bought with money. I may not be a millionaire but I defy the richest man in the world today to show me a similar pearl. Please excuse my words, my friend, but the satisfaction of owning the largest of all pearls is to me worth more than mere money." "In his search for conch shells, he had failed to see the giant Tridacna clam which was

Diver with hand stuck in shell and largest pearl

partly hidden by coral rocks, its huge jaws held open ready to clamp shut with the strength of a bear trap. Etem accidentally got his hand between the shells, which snapped shut, and thus he met his death. With the aid of ropes, the men hoisted their dead comrade and his deep-sea murderer into one of the canoes. The clam was taken to an aged Mohammedan chief and as he watched his men remove the meat from the shell, he suddenly saw an enormous pearl. Seizing it in his hands, he examined the surface and discerned the image of a turbaned face, formed by nature on one of the sides. In this image the Panglima was startled to discover a resemblance to Mohammed. Then as his excited servants stood in awe, the old man prostrated himself before the pearl and began to pray."

Traffic on the Bridge of Spain, spanning the River Pasig, in 1899

The Poor Are Not Far From Sight

"Manila is a city of extremes. The poor are very poor and the rich, very rich. They live side by side. The rich live in sprawling houses in residential sub-divisions with fancy names like Green Meadows, White Plains, Corinthian Plaza, Bel Air, San Lorenzo, Magallanes and the very exclusive Forbes Park, a leafy enclave that was home to the famous Manila Polo Club. The poor are not far from sight. They live in little pockets on the periphery of these affluent subdivisions. A constant reminder to the rich that there is another side to life."

- Arlene J. Chai, in her novel The Last Time I saw Mother, *published in 1997*

Malacanang Palace

The Palacio de Malacañang, the Philippine "White House", has been home to 18 Spanish governors, 14 American governors and numerous Philippine presidents. The name derives from the Tagalog phrase "May lakán diyán", meaning "there is a nobleman there." The structure, first built in 1750, became the official residence of the Spanish governor in 1863 when the original residence in the Intramuros was destroyed by an earthquake.

Grandeur

From Manuel L. Quezon - His Life And Career: A Complete Biography by Sol H. Gwekoh, published in 1948. Quenzoibn, who was President of the Philippines commonwealth – still under nominal US control – from 1935 to 1944 - describes his first visit to the Palace in which he would eventually reside.

In the year 1900, I was privileged for the first time to walk into the grounds of Malacanan and enter the palace halls. The circumstances attending my errand were such that my visit left a lasting vivid impression on my mind. Before that day I had no occasion to see Malacanan even from the street. I knew, of course, of the Palace as the official residence of the Spanish Captain-General who was also the Governor General of the Philippine Islands; and my idea of the grandeur of the palace was in harmony with my conception of the power and authority of the personage occupying it.

144

Balut

A popular street snack in the Philippines is Balut, a bird embryo not fully developed, boiled in the egg shell, for eating. It is often served with beer, and is not recommended for vegetarians.

A Coke ad from the 1950s. Bottled by San Miguel

Yamashita's Gold

Yamashita's gold is the name of the valuables looted by the Japanese in Southeast Asia during the early 1940s, and allegedly collected and hidden in caves in the Philippines. Most experts today think the treasure never existed, but many searches have been made for it, and there are those who believe it is still there somewhere, waiting to be found. It is named after Japanese general Tomoyuki Yamashita, nicknamed "The Tiger of Malaya", who was put in command of Japanese forces in the Philippines in 1944.

In a bizarre development, Imelda Marcos in 1992 claimed the source of the extraordinary wealth possessed by her and her husband was Yamashita's Gold, which she said Ferdinand found in 1945. She said Marcos kept the fortune secret because the amount was so large, "it would be embarrassing." But less embarrassing, it seems, than admitting the riches came from the public coffers.

The Lighthouse

From Pasig: River of Life *by Reynaldo G Alejandro, published in 2000*

"In the days of silent sail-powered ships, the arrival of a schooner or any important vessel was greeted with celestial classics. It was heavenly sound that permeated even the thick walls of the bastion of Santiago, the fort that guarded the river's mouth as the main garrison of Manila."

The Beautiful Lady

The Mayon Volcano on the southeast extension of the island of Luzon, close to the town of Legazpi, is known as having the most perfect cone of any volcano in the world. It is also the most active volcano in the Philippines, and has erupted 49 times in the past 400 years. The name is said to derive from, "Daragang Magayon" in the local language, which means "beautiful lady." The most destructive of the Mayon eruptions began on July 6, 1881 and lasted more than a year.

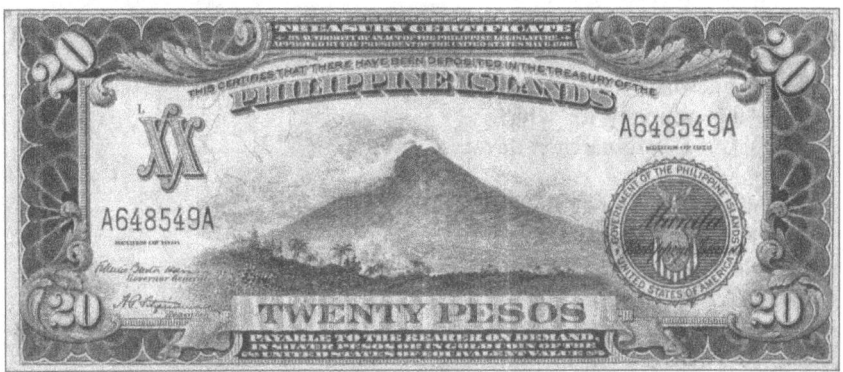

An excerpt from Volcanos and Earthquakes *by Samuel Kneeland*

At the date of my visit, the volcano had poured out, for five months continuously, a stream of lava on the Legaspi side from the very summit. The viscid mass bubbled quietly but grandly, and overran the border of the crater, descending several hundred feet in a glowing wave, like red-hot iron. Gradually, fading as the upper surface cooled, it changed to a thousand sparkling rills among the crevices, and, as it passed beyond the line of complete vision behind the woods near the base, the fires twinkled like stars, or the scintillions of a dying conflagration. More than half of the mountain height was thus illuminated.

Saved Millions, Got Nothing

Dr Abelardo Aguilar was a Filipino physician who helped to discover an importance antibiotic in the early 1950s. But his role in the breakthrough and how it was recognized are in dispute. The discovery of erythromycin undoubtedly saved millions of lives and made the company for which he worked as a researcher, the US pharmaceutical company Eli Lilly and Company, very rich. Aguilar was never paid a single cent as a result of the success of the drug. The story goes like this:

In 1949, Aguilar sent soil samples from Iloilo to his employer, and Eli Lilly's research team, led by J. M. McGuire, isolated erythromycin from the samples. The company in 1952 declared the discovery of a

Dr Abelardo Aguilar

new kind of antibiotic, capable of treating infections without the side-effects of other antibiotics. The drug also worked with people who were allergic to penicillin. The company named the drug Ilosone to commemorate its origin in Iloilo and marketed it under that name worldwide.

Aguilar was promised a trip to the company's manufacturing plant in Indianapolis in recognition of his work, but the trip did not occur. Aguilar left the company and set up his own clinic in Iloilo where he gained the reputation of being a pro-poor doctor. He also tried in vain to get recognition from Eli Lilly. Shortly before his death in 1993, he again wrote the company asking for $500 million in royalties so he could set up a foundation to provide accessible health services to poor Filipinos. As before, his letter was rejected.

Railways

Railways came to the Philippines in 1892 thanks to an Englishman named Don Sykes who obtained approval to build a line from Manila 200 km north to the port city of Dagupan. He transferred the right to the Manila Railroad Co. Ltd, (MRR) a British company, which opened the track on November 24, 1892. When the Americans took over in 1899, another 800 km of lines were laid, but the company suffered big losses, and sold the entire system to the Philippine government in 1916. The railway suffered heavily during the Japanese occupation, partly due to General MacArthur's decision to destroy locomotives and other key facilities before he retreated to Bataan after Pearl Harbor in December 1941. Reconstruction after the war was slow, but in

Manila-railroad-company

1956, it finally turned a profit thanks to the shift from steam to diesel-electric locomotives. The MRR was renamed the Philippine National Railways (PNR) in 1964. It remains today a state-owned and unprofitable rail network.

Ad from the Philippine-Chinese Advocate, Aug 26 1918

Postage Stamps

Stamps issued by the first Philippine Republic between 1899 and 1901, when it was crushed by American forces

Postage stamps issued between 1899 and the 1930s were generally inscribed: "United States of America - Philippine Islands"

A stamp issued by the Japanese occupation forces in the Philippines between 1942 and 1945

The Kingpin of Manila

The toughest and most feared gangster in the history of the Philippines, so far, is Nicasio "Asiong" Rodriguez Salonga, nicknamed the the "Hitler of Tondo" district in Manila. He was shot to death on October 8, 1951 while out drinking with his colleagues. He dominated Manila's crime scene for several years, and while he was linked constantly to cases of extortion, murder, drugs and other such gangster staple activities, he was never arrested. Many in the desperately poor area of Tondo considered him to be a hero. Here was shot at close quarter with a .38 calibre bullet. The motive is unclear, but it was probably on the orders of another gang. Police identified the shooter as Ernesto Reyes, who worked for the Salonga's rival, the gang leader Carlos "Totoy Golem" Capistrano.

A rare photo of Asiong Salonga, Manila's most notorious gangster, gunned down at the age of 26.

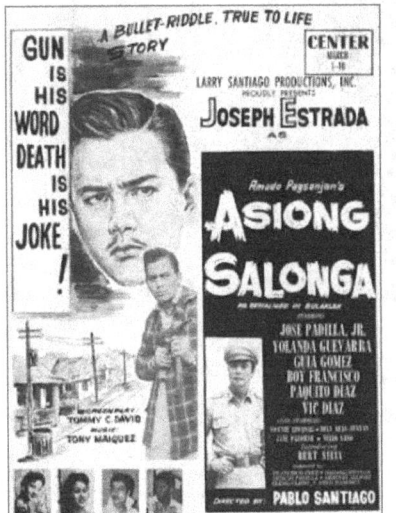

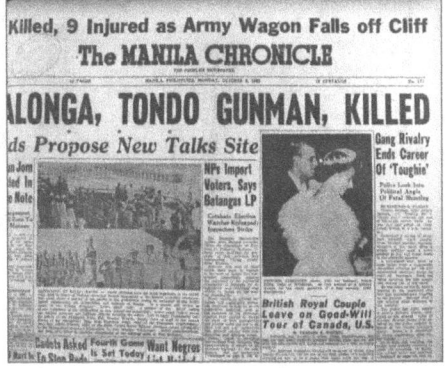

Asiong's life has been re-yun in the movies many times, but the most famous version stars Joseph Estrada, who served as President of the Philippines from 1998 to 2001.

Amalia Fuentes endorsing Coke, 1956

Rizal Avenue in the 1960s. Rizal Avenue, one of Manila's main thoroughfares, was for many years also an important commercial street, but it was hit by the construction of a line of the LRT, the Light Rail system, along the street and the emergence of other commercial centers.

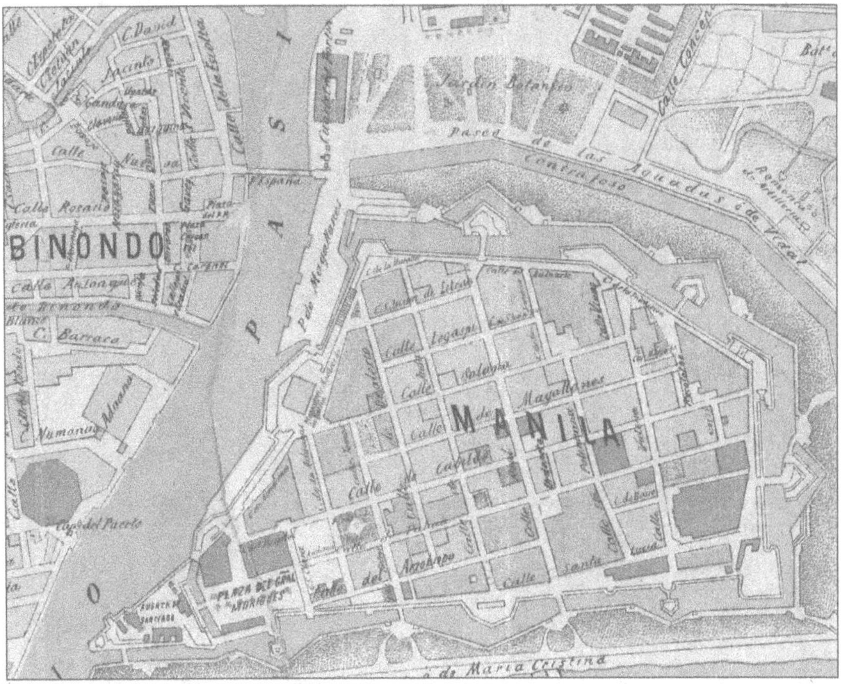

Intramuros Manila 1898

Prestigious Cinema

The film *Anak Dalita* (Child of Sorrow) was a breakthrough. Released in 1956, it was a dark story of murder and prostitution in Manila's slums, very different from the usual entertainment from local studios. The film was directed by Lamberto V. Avellana and won Best Film award at the 1956 Asia Pacific Film Festival.

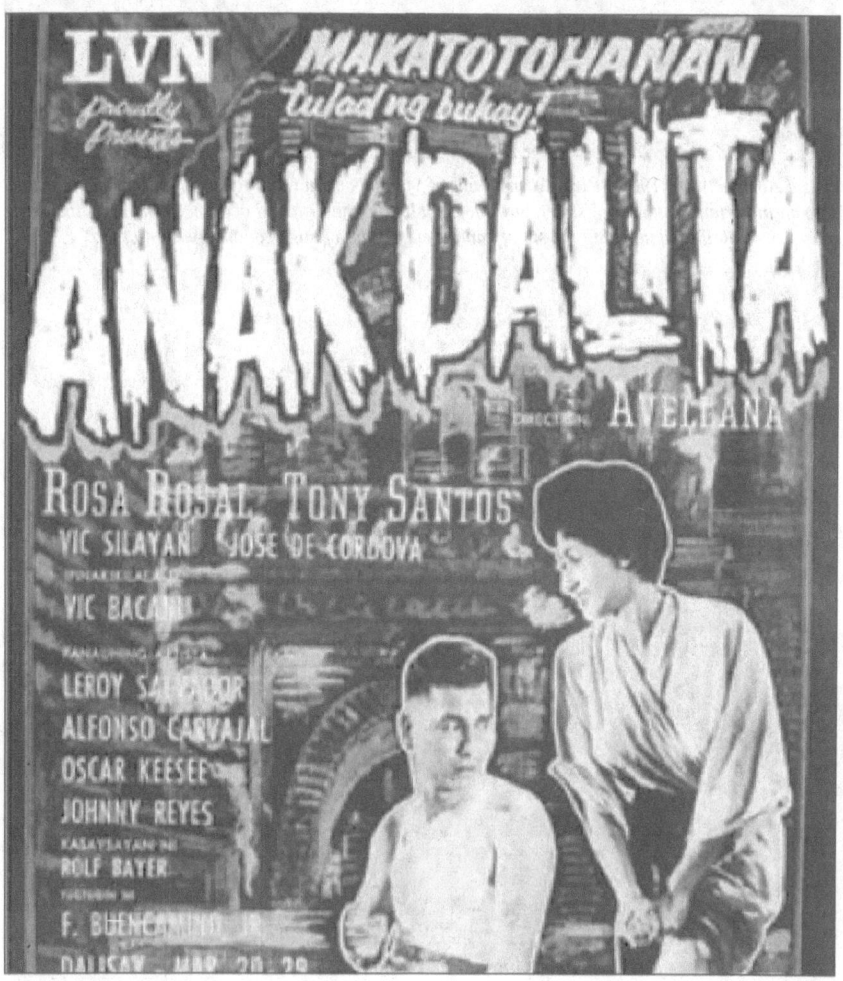

The Last Soldier

Hiroo Onoda was a Japanese soldier who refused to surrender at the end of the war in 1945, and only put down arms in 1974. He was born in 1922 to a samurai warrior family and was posted as an army intelligence officer to Lubang Island in the Philippines in December 1944. He was ordered to do all he could to stop enemy attacks on the island.His orders also stated that under no circumstances was he to surrender or take his own life.

US forces landed on Lubang in February, 1945, and within a short time most of the Japanese troops had either been killed or had surrendered. Onoda ordered the three men under his command to take to the hills with him. One of them walked away in 1949, a second was shot by local police in 1954, and the third was killed by police in 1972. On February 20, 1974, Onoda met a young Japanese traveler named Norio Suzuki, who said he was looking for "Lieutenant Onoda, a panda, and the Abominable Snowman, in that order." Suzuki found Onoda and they became friends, but Onoda still refused to surrender, saying he was waiting for orders from a superior officer.

Suzuki returned to Japan with photographs of himself and Onoda, and the Japanese government found Onoda's commanding officer, Major Yoshimi Taniguchi, by then a bookseller, who flew to Lubang on March 20, 1974, met with Onoda and fulfilled a promise he said made in 1944: "Whatever happens, we'll come back for you." Onoda was thus officially relieved of duty, and he turned over his sword, an operational Japanese rifle, 500 rounds of ammunition and several hand grenades. He died in 2014.

The King of the Road

The basic means of public transport in the Philippines since the 1940s has been the Jeepney, a vehicle originally converted from a huge number of surplus Jeeps left over when most American forces left the country after the Japanese surrender in 1945. Local car repair geniuses stripped them down, added metal roofs and decorated with garish ornaments and in rainbows of color. As the years went by, the chassis on the Jeepney was extended, and benches placed in the back cabin.

A Pan-American Airways advert for China Clipper flights to the Philippines, late 1930s

> *"Filipinos want beauty. I have to look beautiful so that the poor Filipinos will have a star to look at from their slums."*
>
> *- Imelda Marcos*

The Steel Butterfly

Imelda Marcos was born in Manila in 1929 and met politician Ferdinand Marcos in 1954 after a brief career as singer and beauty queen. She married him 11 days later. Ferdinand became president in 1965, which made Imelda the First Lady of the Philippines, a role she reveled in for the next two decades.

Imelda Marcos

Her beauty and poise attracted comparisons to Jackie Kennedy. But the dominant impression of her is still of her lavish lifestyle, in such sharp contrast to the poverty in which so many Filipinos lived then, and still live today. She traveled the world on shopping expeditions, and delighted in hosting banquets for visiting celebrities.

In 1983, opposition politician Benigno Aquino, who had been Imelda's boyfriend at one point in the early 1950s, was assassinated. The Marcos government began to lose its grip and the "People's Power" confrontations in 1986, in which huge crowds demonstrated for change, forced the couple to flee.

They went to Hawaii, leaving most of their possessions behind but taking a large, and largely unrecovered, amount of cash and other assets. Imelda most famously had a huge shoe collection, which she left in the presidential palace.

Ferdinand died in Hawaii 1989, and the government continued efforts to recover the funds. Imelda was charged in the US with fraud and racketeering in connection with this, but was acquitted. In 1991, she returned to the Philippines and at one point ran for president, losing to Fidel V. Ramos. She is known to many in the Philippines by the apt nickname 'Steel Butterfly', She and Ferdinand had three children: Imee, Irene, and Ferdinand Jr., also known as "Bongbong."

> *"They went into my closets looking for skeletons, but thank God, all they found were shoes, beautiful shoes."*
>
> *– Imelda Marcos*

A Marcos supporter holds idealized paintings of his heroes during a rally

Imelda and Ferdinand Marcos visited Beijing in 1974, and met with Chinese leader Mao Zedong, ailing, but still fit enough to kiss Imelda's hand. Imelda was escorted round Beijing by Mao's wife, Jiang Qing.

Marcos speaks from the balcony of the Presidential Palace on February 25, 986, after "winning" his last election. The next day, he had gone.

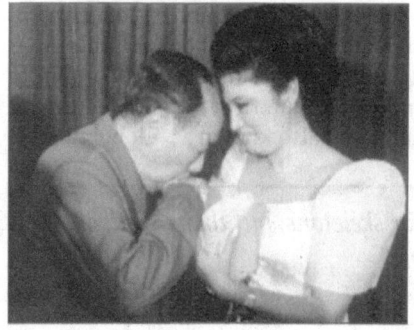

The Marcos Years

Ferdinand Marcos was elected President in 1965, and again for a second term in 1969, but problems with the economy, insurgencies in Luzon and Mindanao and growing student unrest created a crisis that led in 1972 to Marcos declaring Martial Law, which lasted until 1981. During these years, Marcos ruled by decree, abolished Congress, placed tough controls on the media, and ordered the arrest of several opposition leaders, including his main critic Senator Benigno Aquino Jr.

The initial reaction martial law was quite positive, in that it reduced the sense of chaos, but after a while, the abuses by Marcos people and the military resulted in a change in public sentiment. The economy, however, did well during the 1970s. Another presidential election was held in 1981, and the opposition boycotted it, giving Marcos another victory, but the political situation was becoming more unstable. The trigger for changes leading to Marcos' downfall was the assassination of Benigno "Ninoy" Aquino Jr. at Manila International Airport in August 1983 on his return after several years of exile in the United States.

Facing growing pressure, Marcos called a snap election on February 7, 1986 and the opposition was led by Aquino's widow, Corazon Aquino. In a heavily rigged vote, Marcos was declared the winner, the opposition refused to accept the result and some key people withdrew support from Marcos, including General Fidel Ramos. This resulted in the People's Power demonstrations from February 22 to 25, reportedly involving two million people. With demonstrators outside the presidential palace, Marcos decided to flee, and he and his family boarded US Army helicopters which flew him to Clark Air Force base where they changed to US military aircraft that flew them to Guam and then on to Hawaii. Marcos died there in 1989.

> "We Americans like to think we taught the Filipinos democracy. Well, tonight they are teaching the world."
> - *CBS news anchorman Bob Simon*

The Declaration of Martial Law, 1972

Excerpts from the Address of Ferdinand E. Marcos, President of the Philippines, delivered in Malacañang Palace, September 23, 1972.

My countrymen, as of the 21st of this month, I signed Proclamation No. 1081 placing the entire Philippines under martial law. This proclamation was to be implemented upon my clearance and clearance was granted 9 o'clock in the evening of the 22nd, last night. I have proclaimed martial law in accordance with the powers vested in the President by the Constitution of the Philippines. The proclamation of martial law is not a military takeover. I, as your duly elected President of the Republic use this power which may be implemented by the military authorities but still is a power embodied in the Constitution to protect the Republic of the Philippines and our democracy. A republican, a democratic form of government is not helpless government. When it is imperilled by the danger of violent overthrow, an insurrection or a rebellion, it has inherent and built-in powers wisely provided for under the Constitution. Such a danger confronts the Republic of the Philippines. Article 7, Section 10, paragraph 2 of the Constitution provides and I quote: "The President shall be Commander-in-Chief of all Armed Forces of Philippines and whenever it becomes necessary he may call out such armed forces to prevent or suppress lawless violence, invasion, insurrection of rebellion. In case of invasion, insurrection or rebellion or imminent danger thereof, when the public safety requires it, he may suspend the privileges of the writ of habeas corpus or place the Philippines or any part thereof under law." ...

I have also issued General Orders for the government in the meantime to control media and other means of dissemination of information as well as all public utilities .... The carrying of firearms outside residences even if such

firearms are covered by licenses but without the permission of the Armed Forces of the Philippines is punishable by death.

Curfew is established from 12 o'clock midnight to 4 o'clock in the morning. The departure of Filipinos abroad is temporarily suspended. Exceptions, of course, are official missions that may be necessary. Clearances will be given by the Secretary of National Defense.

In the meantime, rallies and demonstrations are prohibited. So, too, are strikes especially in critical public utilities. I have ordered the arrest of those directly involved in the conspiracy to overthrow our duly constituted government by violence and subversion. If you offend the New Society, you shall be punished like the rest of the offenders. Persons who have nothing whatsoever to do with such conspiracy and operations to overthrow the Republic of the Philippines by violence or sub-version have nothing to fear. They can move about and perform their daily activities without any apprehension from action or counteraction by the government especially after the period of counteraction which I have directed to be taken against the conspirators.

I assure you that I am utilizing this power for the proclamation of martial law vested in me by the Constitution for one purpose alone, and that is, to save the Republic and reform our society. I wish to emphasize these two objectives. We will eliminate the threat of a violent overthrow of our Republic, but at the same time, we must now reform the social, economic and political institutions in our country. The plans, the order for reforms and removal of the inequities of our society, the clean-up of government of its corrupt and sterile elements, the liquidation of the criminal syndicates, the systematic development of our economy, the general program for a new and better Philippines will be explained to you. But we must start out with the elimination of anarchy and the maintenance of peace and order.

I have had to use this constitutional power in order that we may not completely lose the civil rights and freedom we cherish. I assure you that this is not a precipitate decision, and that I have weighed all the factors. If there were any other solution at our disposal and within our capability which could solve this problem, we would have utilized such a solution and I would have chosen it. But there was none. I have used the other two alternatives of, first calling out the troops to quell the rebellion and I have suspended the privilege of the writ of habeas corpus. But the rebellion has not been stopped ...

We must now defend the Republic of the Philippines with this stronger power granted by the Constitution. To those guilty of treason, insurrection, rebellion, it may pose a grave danger. But to the ordinary citizens, to almost all of you whose primary concern is merely to be left alone to pursue your lawful activities, this is the guarantee of that freedom that you seek. All that I do is for the Republic and for you.

Here Lies Love

The musician and writer David Byrne, best known for being the lead singer of the band Talking Heads, wrote a musical about Imelda Marcos that was premiered in London 2014. He said he was draws to her story because of the way it highlights the ways in which power influences people, and also because of Imelda's obvious interest in popular music.

"When I heard she had a giant mirror ball in her New York townhouse and turned the roof of the palace in Manila into a dancing club, I thought 'she really surrounded herself with this music and created her own soundtrack to her life," he was quoted by The Guardian as saying.

"The mindset of the Marcos regime and the mindset of disco music to me doesn't seem all that distant," he continued. "The hedonistic, escapist feeling of losing yourself and being transported to another world, like you feel on the dance floor and like you feel in a dance club, that's a means to divorce yourself from the rest of the world, just as Imelda did. When you're dancing, you're in this psychological and sonic bubble, in the same way that powerful people create a bubble around themselves. So I wanted to give an audience a taste of that feeling."

A poster for David Byrne's 2014 musical, based on the life of Imelda Marcos

Canadian-born Lisa Angstadt has traveled
the world and lived and worked in a number
of countries. As a Medical Laboratory
Technologist with a love of reading, she
decided to get into the publishing world.
Merging her love of travel and books, *Tales of
Old Manila* is her first book.